W9-BNH-903

Presented to

On the occasion of

By

Date

✣ *A Catholic Child's* ✤
Illustrated Lives of the Saints

Written by

L.E. McCullough, Ph.D.

Illustrated by

William Luberoff

and

Robert Berran

Regina
Press

Nihil Obstat: Reverend Robert O. Morrisey, J.C.D.
                    Censor librorum
                    August 8th, 2002

Imprimatur: Most Reverend William Murphy
                    Bishop of Rockville Centre
                    September 12, 2002

*Dedicated to the memory of P.J. Becker,
who is now with the saints in heaven.*

THE REGINA PRESS
10 Hub Drive
Melville, New York 11747

All rights reserved. No part of this publication may be reproduced or transmitted in any form or by any means, electronic or mechanical, including photocopying, recording, or any information storage and retrieval system, without permission in writing from the publishers.

© Copyright 2002, 2005 by The Regina Press
Artwork © 2002, 2005 Reproducta, NY

ISBN 0-88271-140-7

Printed in Hong Kong.

Table of Contents

Foreword

Having lived in over thirty "permanent" residences during the course of my life, my personal possessions have scattered hither and yon like falling leaves in a high wind. One of the very few items I retain from my childhood is a book, the *Lives of the Saints*, given to me by my Grandmother and Grandfather McCullough on the occasion of my Communion at St. Michael's Catholic Church, Indianapolis, Indiana.

I loved this book when I received it at seven years of age, and I love it now. I loved it then because of its exciting and seemingly incredible stories about heroic men and women from other times, other places. I love it now because I have come to realize that the stories of these long ago, faraway saints have as much meaning in our world as it did in theirs.

The lives of the Catholic Saints provide ready-made role models for children seeking moral instruction and support. Their stories are an extension of the parables Jesus told to his disciples. Yet, the saints' lives are not abstract allegories; they are the record of what real people did to aid their fellow humans in moving this earth ever closer to the Paradise intended by our Creator.

For today's children, saints are genuine "action figures" — men and women, often boys and girls — whose faith in the teachings of Jesus Christ was continuously tested, sometimes every minute of the day. Saints were often imperfect. They were subject to doubt, fear, losing their way. But in the end, with the help of God's grace and their own indomitable courage and free will, they triumphed over the obstacles and temptations that might otherwise have kept them from attaining a state of true holiness.

Saints knew that their life mattered in the overall scheme of things. They knew that each prayer, each good deed, each pious thought had value in God's plan for the universe. Our children need to know that their lives matter. They may not be asked to lay down their life as a martyr, but the day-to-day decisions they will make as students — and later as parents, workers, citizens — are crucial to the foundation of a God-centered world.

Saints cared for other people. They became "little Christs" who did whatever was in their power to heal, to console, to ease suffering. Even saints who chose a life of retreat and silence saw the ultimate purpose of their lives as a service to God and, hence, to humanity. By following the saints' example of service to others, our children can be inspired to begin the habit of thinking beyond their own desires. . . to think globally and act locally and personally in making their immediate environment more Christ-filled and more sensitive to the needs of others.

The lives of the Catholic Saints demonstrate that anyone can be a saint, any place, any time. That's probably why I still have that book my grandparents gave me. And always will have it. To keep reminding me each and every day that, if I want to meet a real-life saint, all I have to do is look in the mirror.

L.E. McCullough, Ph.D.
Woodbridge, New Jersey

What is a Saint?

The meaning of the word "saint" in Hebrew, Greek and Latin is "holy one." A saint is a person who is considered holy, sanctified or consecrated by means of having lived a life of great charity and heroic virtues.

The Catholic Church has designated three steps to full sainthood.

First, a person is declared *Venerable*. This is a deceased person recognized as having lived a life filled with heroic virtues.

Second, a person is declared *Blessed*, or "beatified." In addition to personal attributes of charity and heroic virtue, one miracle acquired through the individual's intercession is required.

Third, a person is declared a *Saint*, or "canonized." Proof of two miracles are required, though a Pope may waive these requirements. Martyrdom for the faith does not usually require a miracle.

All Saints Day is a feast that remembers all Christian saints, known and unknown. It is celebrated by the Roman Catholic Church on November 1 and by Orthodox Catholics on the first Sunday after Pentecost.

*S*aint Mary, as you helped the child Jesus grow up to become the Savior of the World, help me grow into the adult I must be to best serve God.

Saint Mary,
Mother of God & Queen of Saints

*E*ven before her birth, Mary was destined for a special role in God's plan for humankind. She was born free from original sin, the only child of Anne and Joachim. As a young girl, she entered the Temple and took a vow of virginity. A few years later, while living in Nazareth, Mary was visited by the archangel Gabriel. The archangel told her she would become the Mother of Jesus by the Holy Spirit. Guided by her faith, Mary married the carpenter Joseph. Mary gave birth to Jesus in a humble stable at Bethlehem.

Mary was often with Jesus during his public ministry. She was responsible for inspiring Him to perform His first miracle, when she noticed the wedding feast at Cana had run out of wine. And, when her Son died upon the Cross, she was standing faithfully below. Mary was also present at the Ascension and Pentecost.

Since ancient times, Mary has appeared to thousands of people all over the world, throughout Europe, Asia, Africa, Australia and North and South America, holding out the promise of eternal love and hope. More than fifty days in the Catholic calendar of feasts are devoted to Mary including her birth (September 8), her Assumption into heaven (August 15), her Immaculate Conception (December 8) and the Annunciation by the Angel Gabriel that she would bear the Son of God (March 25).

Mary was given the honor of bringing the Son of God into the world. She also suffered great pain in seeing Him die for the world's sins. As Mary stayed with Jesus until He left the earth, she remains at our side, too, from birth until death, while we struggle with the hardships and challenges of life.

*S*aint Elizabeth Seton, as you did not let illness or sadness stop
you from bringing the joy of Christ to others, help me carry God's
message to wherever it is needed.

Saint Elizabeth Seton Feast Day: January 4

*E*lizabeth Bayley was born in New York in 1774, the daughter of a wealthy Episcopal family. As a child, she loved to read. The Bible was one of her favorite books.

When she was nineteen, she married Will Seton. Elizabeth and Will had five children and were a happy family until Will died of tuberculosis on a trip to Italy in 1803. For years Elizabeth had felt a deep interest in Catholicism. Now in Italy, Elizabeth and her children drew great solace from the churches of Italy and from the company of Catholic families. Elizabeth asked the Blessed Virgin to guide her to the True Faith. She became a Catholic on Ash Wednesday, 1805.

Elizabeth went to Baltimore and started the first free Catholic school in America in 1809, St. Joseph's School for Girls next to the chapel of St. Mary's Seminary. That same year, Elizabeth became a nun and founded the Sisters of Charity. This was the first native American religious community for women and was based on the Daughters of Charity established by St. Vincent de Paul in France.

The Sisters of Charity were very active and established schools, hospitals and orphanages. Besides her responsibilities to the Order, Elizabeth Seton worked with the sick and poor, composed music and hymns, and wrote spiritual books.

Elizabeth died of tuberculosis in 1821. She said, "We know that God gives us every grace, every abundant grace; and though we are so weak of ourselves, this grace is able to carry us through every obstacle and difficulty. We know certainly that our God calls us to a holy life."

Elizabeth Seton was the first native born American to be canonized by the Catholic Church. She is the patron saint of widows. The Basilica of the National Shrine of St. Elizabeth Ann Seton is in Emmitsburg, Maryland, where Elizabeth Seton lived for several years until her death.

*S*aint John Neumann, you used the power of the mind to spread
knowledge of Jesus' works. Help me use my God-given intellect
to lead others on a heavenly path.

Saint John Neumann

John Neumann was born in Bohemia in 1811. He came to New York in 1836 at a time when there very few priests in America — only thirty-six priests for 200,000 Catholics in New York and New Jersey alone. He was given the choice of serving in the city of Buffalo or of taking charge of the untamed rural areas in Western New York. John chose the more difficult countryside.

For the next twenty years, John Neumann traveled throughout the Eastern United States, making sure Catholics stayed in touch with their faith. He often lived on bread and water and walked miles to visit farm after remote farm. He built fifty churches and opened almost one hundred schools, many of them made from logs. A talented linguist, he was able to hear confessions in twelve languages. He was appointed Bishop of Philadelphia in 1852, and it was there he began the first system of diocesan schools for Catholic students.

John Neumann was the founder of the first national parish for Italians in the United States. He was also a member of the Redemptorists, an order that follows the example of Jesus Christ the Redeemer by preaching the word of God to the poor. In 1840 he became a citizen of the United States and is the first American man and first American bishop to be canonized. The National Shrine of St. John Neumann is in Philadelphia, Pennsylvania.

John Neumann said, "Since every man of whatever race is endowed with the dignity of a person, he has an inalienable right to an education corresponding to his proper destiny and suited to his native talents, his cultural background, and his ancestral heritage." John Neumann's belief in education as a powerful tool for bringing humankind closer to God led to his becoming the first American bishop to be canonized.

*S*aint Francis de Sales, your power as a soldier of God lay in your meekness and humility. Help me forgive and excuse the unkindnesses of others.

Saint Francis de Sales *Feast Day: January 24*

*B*orn in 1567 in Savoy, Francis de Sales was a successful lawyer. One night, he heard a voice saying, "Leave all and follow Me." After much prayer, Francis de Sales realized this was Jesus speaking to him, and he quickly gave up law for the priesthood.

Francis de Sales volunteered to go to a part of Switzerland where Catholics had forsaken their faith for the Calvinist religion. It was a dangerous mission that put his life in danger. Yet, people were won over by his kindness and his clear explanations of Catholic doctrine. More than 70,000 Calvinists returned to the Catholic Church because of Francis de Sales. "We are not drawn to God by iron chains," he said, "but by sweet attractions and holy inspirations."

In 1602 Francis de Sales became Bishop of Geneva. He immediately began religious instruction for the faithful, both young and old. He visited all the parishes scattered across the many mountains of his diocese and helped reform the monasteries and convents. His sermons were very powerful, and he wrote many articles about faith. Most importantly, in an age where many religious leaders were angry and intolerant, Francis de Sales was humble and gentle. His calm manner drew many people to him and to the Church.

Francis de Sales had a great love for the poor. "Nothing makes us so prosperous in this world as to give alms. It is to those who have the most need of us that we ought to show our love more especially." In 1610 Francis de Sales helped St. Jeanne de Chantal form the Visitation Sisters.

The patron saint of journalists, Francis de Sales died of a heart attack in 1622. His last words were, "God's will be done! Jesus, my God and my all!"

*S*aint Thomas Aquinas, you used the power of the human mind to understand the glory of heaven. Help me grow in my understanding of God's plan for the world.

Saint Thomas Aquinas Feast Day: January 28

*T*homas Aquinas was one of the greatest scholars the Church has ever known. His master work, *Summa Theologica*, combined wisdom of the ancient world with the new message of Christianity. It explained the principles of Catholic faith so even the most unlearned person could easily understand. Said Thomas Aquinas, "Charity is the form, mover, mother and root of all the virtues."

Thomas Aquinas was born in Naples, Italy, in 1225. A holy hermit foretold his career, saying to his mother before his birth: "He will enter the Order of Friars Preachers, and so great will be his learning and sanctity that in his day no one will be found to equal him."

At the age of five, Thomas Aquinas was sent to receive his first training from the Benedictine monks of Monte Cassino. He was diligent in study and devoted to prayer. His teachers were surprised at hearing the child ask frequently, "What is God?" and other questions indicating a deep interest in philosophy.

Thomas Aquinas studied at the major universities of Europe and obtained the degree of Doctor in Theology from the University of Paris. Because of his quiet manner and large size, other students called him "the dumb Sicilian ox." One day he astonished the class with a brilliant explanation of a difficult passage. Said his teacher, "We have called Thomas 'dumb ox,' but I tell you his bellowing will yet be heard to the uttermost parts of the earth."

Thomas Aquinas was loved for his kindness and willingness to share his knowledge. Prayer, he said, had taught him more about the world than study. "Grant me, O Lord my God, a mind to know you, a heart to seek You, wisdom to find You, conduct pleasing to You, faithful perseverance in waiting for You and a hope of finally embracing You."

Thomas Aquinas died in 1274 while on the way to a meeting with the Pope. He is the patron saint of students and of learning and of all Catholic universities throughout the world.

*S*aint John Bosco, as you saw Jesus in the face of every child, help me show kindness to the strangers I meet.

Saint John Bosco *Feast Day: January 31*

John Bosco grew up in a poor Italian farm family in the 1820s. To earn extra money, he would present magic shows for other children — only if they promised to pray with him before and after the show.

During his school days, John Bosco worked as a tailor, a baker, a shoemaker and a carpenter. After much hard work and study, John Bosco was ordained a priest and taught at an orphanage in Turin. He devoted his spare time to finding poor children in the city slums. He entertained them with stories and tricks and found them jobs. He wrote many articles and books explaining the teachings of Christ. Then he showed his young listeners how to print them for themselves.

John Bosco knew it was important for adults to take responsibility for wayward children. "Let us regard those boys over whom we have some authority as our own sons," he wrote. "Let us place ourselves in their service." He founded the Salesians of Don Bosco, an order of priests who educate boys. To aid abandoned girls, he founded the Daughters of Mary, Help of Christians. For lay people, he founded the Union of Cooperator Salesians.

John Bosco believed greatly in the power of Holy Communion. He wrote, "Do you want our Lord to give you many graces? Visit Him often. Do you want Him to give you few graces? Visit Him seldom. Visits to the Blessed Sacrament are powerful and indispensable means of overcoming the attacks of the devil. Make frequent visits to Jesus in the Blessed Sacrament, and the devil will be powerless against you."

John Bosco died in 1888 and is the patron saint of boys and apprentices.

$\mathcal{S}$aint Katharine Drexel, you gave away all of your worldly wealth to help spread the word of God. Help us learn how to use our talents wisely in this world to give aid and comfort to others.

Saint Katherine Drexel

Saint Katharine Drexel was born in Philadelphia in 1858 to a very wealthy family who taught her that good fortune was a gift from God to be used to help others. Her parents hosted a Sunday School for poor children, and her two sisters founded schools for orphans and the poor.

Katharine was very interested in the welfare of Native Americans in the West. One day Katharine asked Pope Leo XIII to send more missionaries to Wyoming to help them. The pope replied, "Why don't you become a missionary?"

This is exactly what Saint Katharine Drexel did. She became a nun and then received permission to found the Sisters of the Blessed Sacrament in 1891, an order with the sole purpose of teaching Native Americans and African Americans, who were not then receiving equal educational opportunities. In just a few years, the Sisters of the Blessed Sacrament had created 63 schools in 13 states, nearly 100 missions and a college — Xavier University in New Orleans, the first Catholic African American University in the United States.

Sister Katharine Drexel was not content with simply teaching the Catholic faith. She tried to make others feel responsible for their fellow human beings and change the social conditions that bred poverty and illness. She said, "The patient and humble endurance of the cross whatever nature it may be is the highest work we have to do. If we live the Gospel, we will be people of justice and our lives will bring the good news to the poor."

Katherine Drexel died in 1955 in Bensalem, Pennsylvania. She was beatified on November 20, 1988 by Pope John Paul II and canonized by him on October 1, 2000.

$\mathcal{S}$aint Patrick, *you forgave those who harmed you and patiently taught them the love of Christ. Help me to forgive my enemies and work to bring God into their lives.*

Saint Patrick Feast Day: March 17

*B*orn in 387 A.D., Patrick was the son of a prominent Roman family that lived in Scotland. When he was sixteen, he was kidnapped from his home by pagan pirates who took him to Ireland. There he lived as a slave for many years until escaping. Instead of anger, Patrick felt love for his captors. He vowed to return and convert the Irish people to Christianity.

During the next thirty years, that is exactly what Patrick did. He studied for the priesthood in France and was sent by the Pope in 433 to Christianize Ireland. As a captive, Patrick had learned to speak the Irish language, and he became familiar with the teachings of the Druids, the priests whose pagan religion he would replace with Christianity.

He traveled throughout Ireland, to the farthest parts of the island, preaching the word of Christ. He baptized all the Irish kings and their subjects. When addressing the high king of Ireland on Easter Sunday, he used a humble native flower, the shamrock, with its triple leaf and single stem to explain the doctrine of the Holy Trinity.

Many miracles are associated with St. Patrick. One time a chieftain drew his sword to kill Patrick, but his arm suddenly became paralyzed and was not healed until he converted to Christianity. Another time a Druid priest caused a cloud of darkness to spread over the country, but Patrick's prayers let the sunlight break through.

Patrick founded three monasteries and filled the countryside with churches and schools of learning and worship. He ordained many priests and consecrated no fewer than 350 bishops.

The memory of his good works is so strong that, even today, people in Ireland talk about him as if he had died just a few years ago instead of in the fifth century. He died on March 17, which is his feast day. It is said that on the day he died, no darkness fell and that never again were the nights as dark as they had been before.

*S*aint Joseph, as you were always obedient to the will of God, help me clearly see the course of life God has planned for me.

Saint Joseph

Joseph was Jesus' foster father and a simple carpenter, the one man among all men chosen by God to aid Mary in helping Jesus grow to manhood. "Joseph, son of David, fear not to take unto thee Mary thy wife," an angel of God said to Joseph, "for that which is conceived in her, is of the Holy Ghost. . . And Joseph, rising from his sleep, did as the angel of the Lord had commanded him, and took unto him his wife."

Joseph accepted this responsibility without questioning God. He was ready to fulfill whatever task was required of him. Even though Mary was due to give birth to Jesus, Joseph obediently followed the Roman law ordering the head of each Jewish household to journey to his birthplace and be counted in the census.

After Jesus was born, another angel of God warned Joseph of King Herod's plan to kill all newborn Jewish boys. Joseph was told to flee to safety in Egypt, and he did so. The Holy Family stayed there for several years, until another angel told them it was safe to return to Israel.

Joseph was a kind, patient father and took good care of Mary and Jesus. Years later, when twelve-year-old Jesus went to Jerusalem without telling anyone, Joseph immediately searched for Him. He did not rest until he found his son in the Temple, lecturing to the high priests.

Though he was a simple working man, Joseph was descended from David, the greatest king of Israel. This nobility of character was important, because Joseph lived a life of obedience to God, cherishing faith in the word and will of God.

Joseph is the patron saint of fathers, carpenters, the universal Church and those who work for social justice. He has two feast days: March 19 for Joseph the Husband of Mary and May 1 for Joseph the Worker.

*J*ohn Baptist de LaSalle, you gave the gift of God's learning to so many. Help me use my knowledge to further God's teachings on earth.

Saint John Baptist de LaSalle   *Feast Day: April 7*

John Baptist de LaSalle was was born in 1651 in Rheims, France, the eldest of eleven children. When his parents died, he left the seminary to care for his brothers and sisters. After they had grown, he returned to school and was ordained a priest.

John Baptist de LaSalle believed all children must receive quality education, not just the rich. He knew that ignorance was a breeding ground for evil thoughts and deeds. He also realized that good Christian education depended upon having good teachers.

In 1680 John Baptist de LaSalle founded the Brothers of the Christian Schools (Christian Brothers) to provide teachers for the poor. Soon, even the wealthy wanted their sons to attend John Baptist de LaSalle's schools. He began the first teachers' colleges and was also the first to set up a reform school for delinquent boys. Today, there are over 20,000 Christian Brothers teaching 750,000 students in eighty-five countries.

John Baptist de LaSalle created many new ways of teaching. He was the first to divide students into classes according to their stage of mental abilities. He introduced the blackboard and expanded subjects of study to include ethics, literature, physics, philosophy and mathematics. He also believed that students should learn in their own native language as well as Latin.

Most importantly, John Baptist de LaSalle saw the school as a community of faith. He wrote that teachers were "ambassadors of Christ" and "ministers of grace."

John Baptist de LaSalle spent most of his family fortune on starting schools. What he had left, he gave to the poor of Rheims during the Great Famine of 1683. He died on Good Friday and is the patron saint of school principals and teachers of all youth.

*S*aint Bernadette, you never doubted the word of Mary. Help me hear God's voice in the ordinary things around me.

Saint Bernadette

*B*ernadette was born in 1844 at Lourdes, in the Pyrenees Mountains of France. Her parents were very poor and she herself was in poor health. When she was fourteen years old, she was walking in the woods near a spring. She heard a noise like a gust of wind and saw a light. In the light, Bernadette saw a young girl dressed in white, with a blue sash around her waist, a yellow rose on each foot and rosary beads on her arm. It was the Virgin Mary.

"I am the Immaculate Conception," said Mary. Bernadette fell to her knees and began praying the rosary. The Blessed Virgin appeared to Bernadette seventeen more times. She told Bernadette to pray for sinners, do penance and have a chapel built there in the honor of Mary.

When Bernadette told people of her visions, no one in the village believed her. Then Our Lady told Bernadette to dig in the dried mud near the mouth of a cave. As she dug, a spring of water burst forth from the ground, and water began to flow. Our Lady told Bernadette to let people know that the waters of the spring had healing powers, if coupled with great faith in God.

With each day the spring grew ever larger. Many miracles happened when people began to use this water. A man who had lost an eye recovered his sight when he washed his face in the spring water. A child who was dying was restored to health after he walked in the spring.

Over the years, more miracles took place, and the Catholic Church recognized Lourdes as a holy place. Each year five million people from around the world travel to Lourdes, hoping to experience the healing power of God.

Bernadette joined the Sisters of Charity and died in 1879. Of her special place in history, she said simply, "Jesus is for me honor, delight, heart and soul."

*S*aint George, you offered your life for others as did Jesus on the cross. Help me always make the right choice when faced with challenges to my faith.

Saint George

Feast Day: April 23

The patron saint of soldiers, the Boy Scouts and England, George was born in Israel of Christian parents in the third century. He joined the Roman Army and was promoted to tribune by Emperor Diocletian.

When Diocletian began to persecute Christians, George knew what he had to do. He criticized the emperor and resigned from the army. "I am a Christian," said George, "and nothing can shake my faith." George gave away all his worldly wealth to the poor and prepared to join the Army of Christ. He was tortured and beheaded, but his courage in the face of certain death inspired many conversions and many tales of miracles.

The most famous story is when George saved a village from a ferocious dragon that lived near a lake in North Africa. Entire armies had tried to kill this fierce creature, and all had been defeated and killed. The dragon devoured two sheep each day. If a sheep could not be found, the villagers were forced to give up one of their daughters.

George arrived in the village and heard the woeful tale of evil. A young girl was about to be given to the dragon, but George told her to wait. He crossed himself with the Sign of the Cross and rode to battle against the dragon, killing it with a single blow of his lance. George gave thanks to God for his victory, and many villagers were converted to Christianity. George received a rich reward and gave it to the poor.

George is included among the Fourteen Holy Helpers. These are a group of saints known to give special protection and include besides George, Sts. Achatius, Barbara, Blaise, Catherine of Alexandria, Christopher, Cyriacus, Denis, Erasmus, Eustachius, Giles, Margaret of Antioch, Pantaleon and Vitus.

*S*aint Mark, as you overcame your fear of committing to Christ, help me remain steadfast in my journey along God's path.

Saint Mark

*T*he first time Mark appears in the Bible is at the mention of a young man who ran away when Jesus was arrested. After Jesus' Resurrection, Mark conquered his fear and became a Christian in his home city of Jerusalem. He traveled as a missionary preaching the word of Christ with his cousin, St. Barnabas, and with St. Paul.

When Mark arrived in Rome, he was asked to set down the teachings of the first Pope, St. Peter. His writings became the second Gospel of the New Testament, a book that records the life of Jesus as seen through the eyes of St. Peter.

In Mark's gospel there is a lot of information about Jesus' ministry. Mark shows the human side of Jesus. He lets us see Jesus when he is angry, happy, sad and hopeful. He shows us many miracles of Jesus as he walked among the people of Israel, trying to fire their imagination with the wonders and possibilities of heaven: raising up Peter's mother-in-law, healing Jairus' daughter, curing a man with demons, calming the stormy waters of the sea, multiplying the loaves and fishes.

Mark tells us that Jesus said, "I tell you whatever you ask for in prayer, believe that you receive it, and you will."

Most importantly, the gospel of Mark shows how the terrible suffering of Jesus during his trial and crucifixion led to glory and salvation with the coming of God's kingdom. He lets us hear the words of the centurions at the Cross when they realize who they have killed: "Truly this man was the Son of God!"

It is believed that Mark founded the first Christian church in Alexandria and spread Christianity throughout Egypt. He is the patron of notaries and lawyers.

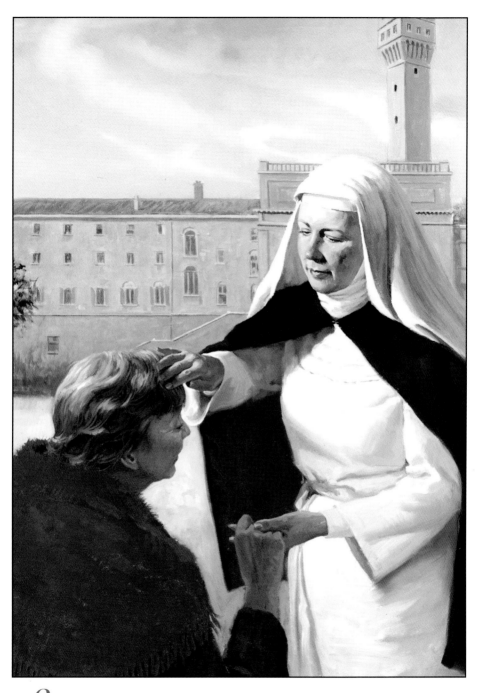

*S*aint Catherine of Siena, you rose to the defense of the Church when needed. Help me prove strong when my faith is tested.

Saint Catherine of Siena

At the age of six, Catherine of Siena had a vision in which Jesus appeared and blessed her. From then on she devoted herself to becoming a guardian and guide of the Church. When she was fifteen, she joined the Dominican Order of nuns.

Yet, Catherine of Siena's life was not to be one of quiet reflection and prayer. The 14th century was a time of great conflict within the Church. On a mission of unity and peace, Catherine of Siena traveled through Italy, convincing rebellious cities and states not to abandon Christianity.

At that time, the Pope did not live in Rome. He had moved to France and was controlled by the King of France. Catherine went to see the Pope and told him that the seat of the Church belonged in Rome, where St. Peter had founded it. "Holy Father," she said, "your place is in Rome. Come home to your people." Moved by her simplicity and power of faith, the Pope obeyed and moved the Church back to Rome.

Catherine of Siena was not afraid to express her beliefs on the important social issues of the day. She convinced many priests who were living in luxury to give away their riches to the poor and to live more simply. Catherine of Siena became counselor to the Pope and spoke out strongly against a group of disloyal cardinals who had elected an anti-pope.

Catherine of Siena wrote a book called *The Dialog*, in which she told of her visions and other spiritual experiences. "Everything comes from love, all is ordained for the salvation of man," she said. "God does nothing without this goal in mind. Charity is the sweet and holy bond which links the soul with its Creator: it binds God with man and man with God." Catherine of Siena died at age thirty-three of a sudden, mysterious illness. She is the patron saint against fire and bodily ills.

$\mathcal{S}$aint Philip, you saw the divine light of Jesus at first glance.
Open my eyes to His presence in our world today.

Saint Philip

*P*hilip was one of the first chosen disciples of Jesus. Married and the father of several children, Philip was an ordinary man living in Galilee. One day a stranger passed him on the road and said, "Follow Me."

The stranger was Jesus, but Philip saw right away He was the Son of God. Filled with faith, Philip obeyed Jesus' command and left his home to join the twelve men whose belief and courage would change the course of world history.

Soon after Philip met his friend Nathaniel. "We have found Him of whom Moses and the prophets wrote," said Philip. "Who?" asked Nathaniel. "Jesus of Nazareth," replied Philip.

Nathaniel was surprised and asked, "Can any good come out of Nazareth?" Philip answered simply, "Come and see," and brought Nathaniel to Jesus. Like Philip, Nathaniel immediately knew he was in the presence of the Messiah when he met Jesus, and he joined the disciples without delay.

Philip's belief in Jesus was very strong. When Jesus spoke of His Father in heaven, Philip cried out, "Lord, show us the Father, and it is enough!" Jesus replied, "He who sees Me, sees the Father also."

Philip preached Christ's message of salvation for several years in Greece and Asia Minor until 80 A.D. when he, like Jesus, was crucified, for his belief. He is the patron saint of Luxembourg and Uruguay.

*S*aint James, you helped guide the early Christians along a holy path. Help me see the truth of God's teachings with every step I take.

Saint James

A cousin of Jesus, James was also one of the original disciples and the brother of Saint Jude. His mother Mary was a sister of the Blessed Virgin, and for that reason, according to Jewish custom, James is sometimes called the brother of the Lord.

Because of his loyalty to Jesus, James was favored by a special apparition of Christ after the Resurrection, which convinced him all the more that the decision to give up his life as a fisherman to follow Christ was the will of God.

After the Apostles left Israel to preach the word of Christ among the nations, James stayed in the Holy Land to serve the new Church as Bishop of Jerusalem. James wrote an epistle that gave advice to people trying to give up pagan gods for the Christian faith. He encouraged them to stay strong in their faith in spite of persecution and to remember that faith alone would not save them unless they practiced good works.

"Religion that is pure and undefiled before God and the Father is this: to visit orphans and widows in their afflictions, and to keep oneself unstained from the world. My brethren, if any one among you wanders from the truth and someone brings him back, let him know that whoever brings back a sinner from the error of his way will save his soul from death and will cover a multitude of sins."

Saint James practiced great purity in his private life, drinking no wine and wearing no sandals. He often knelt in prayer for so long that the skin on his knees became as hardened as a camel's hoof. It is said that the Jews, out of respect for his holiness, would touch the hem of his garment.

However, after almost thirty years of peacefully preaching among the people of Jerusalem, he angered a mob of idol-worshippers. James was stoned to death in 62 A.D., yet prayed for his killers with the same words Jesus spoke on the cross: "Heavenly Father, forgive them, they know not what they do."

*S*aint Florian, you were not afraid to protect the weak. Help me be ready to offer assistance to those who need my aid.

Saint Florian

*T*he patron saint of firefighters, Florian was a Roman army officer in Austria during the third century in the reign of the Emperor Diocletian, a terrible persecutor of Christians. Well-known for his bravery, it is said Florian stopped a town from burning by throwing a single bucket of water on the blaze.

One day Florian was ordered to execute a group of Christians. He refused and proclaimed that he, too, was a follower of Christ. When the prefect Aquilinus demanded he sacrifice to the pagan gods or be killed, Florian replied, "You do indeed possess power over my body, but you cannot touch my soul. For God alone prevails there. I have obeyed your commands in so far as it befits a soldier, but no one persuades me to offer sacrifice to demons."

Florian was tortured and sentenced by the prefect to be burnt to death. Florian stood on the pile of wood and challenged the Roman soldiers to start the fire. He said, "If you do, I will climb to heaven on the flames."

Fearful of Florian and the power of his Christian God, the prefect ordered him to be drowned instead. A soldier threw Florian into the river, and immediately the soldier's eyes fell from his head. Florian's body was raised up on the waves and washed up on a rock, where it was protected by an eagle with its wings spread in the shape of a cross.

Later, Florian's body was recovered and buried by a devout woman. It was then removed to a monastery, near Linz, where many miracles attributed to him began to occur. He is also invoked in prayers against damage from water and flooding and from drowning.

$\mathcal{S}$aint Peregrine, your faith changed the lives of thousands. Help my faith grow until it, too, becomes a force for good in my world.

Saint Peregrine

*B*orn in Italy in 1260, Peregrine began life as a person very unlikely to become a saint. His family belonged to a political party that rebelled against the Pope. When the Pope's prior general, St. Philip Benizi, came to speak about ending the dispute, Peregrine insulted and heckled him. Peregrine became so angry, that he actually struck Philip. When Philip offered the other cheek for striking, Peregrine was so overcome that he repented and converted to Catholicism.

This moment of violence changed Pergerine's life. From that day on, he stopped worrying about politics and began doing good works for the poor of his town. He joined an order of monks, the Servants of Mary, and spent the next fifty years dedicating himself to helping the sick and the poor. Like St. Paul, another saint who had criticized the Catholic Church before his conversion, Peregrine's early defiance made him one of the most powerful preachers of the Gospel, and he brought many people back to the Church.

To atone for his previous bad conduct, Peregrine imposed a peculiar penance upon himself — he would stand whenever possible, rather than sit. This habit caused a bad case of varicose veins, and one of Peregrine's legs became an open running sore that was diagnosed as cancer. The night before the surgeon was to cut off the diseased leg, Peregrine prayed before the crucifix for many hours. Peregrine believed he saw Christ come down from the crucifix and touch his leg. When Peregrine awoke the next morning, the leg was completely healed and the cancer gone.

Peregrine spent the next twenty-five years until his death continuing to do good works. He is the patron saint of those afflicted with cancer, AIDS and other serious diseases.

*S*aint Dominic Savio, your passion for the love of Jesus made you impervious to slights and slanders. Help me keep my thoughts on the rewards of heaven.

Saint Dominic Savio

*O*ne of ten children, Dominic Savio began serving at Mass when he was five years old. On his First Communion, he resolved to die rather than ever commit a sin, so strongly did he feel the call of God.

Dominic entered an Oratory School at age twelve with the hope of becoming a priest. His strong moral character impressed everyone. Once, two boys filled the school stove with snow. When the teacher came back into the room, they falsely accused Dominic Savio. Dominic Savio refused to tell on the two boys and was punished. After the truth was discovered, the teacher asked Dominic Savio why he didn't proclaim his innocence. He said that he was imitating Jesus, who remained silent during His persecutions.

Dominic Savio said, "Nothing seems tiresome or painful when you are working for a Master who pays well, who rewards even a cup of cold water given for love of Him. I am not capable of doing big things, but I want to do everything, even the smallest things, for the greater glory of God."

Another time Dominic Savio broke up a vicious stone fight between two boys. He held up a crucifix and said, "This is Friday, the day Christ died for love of us. Can you look at Him and still hate each other?"

Sadly, Dominic Savio never achieved his dream of becoming a priest. He died of an illness at age fifteen. His last words were, "What beautiful things I see!"

Dominic Savio's birthplace is now a retreat house for teenagers. The home where he grew up is now a retreat home for children. He is the patron saint of choir boys and of the falsely accused.

*S*aint Isidore the Farmer, you offered your labor to God as a daily prayer. Help me do my chores and schoolwork knowing they please God.

Saint Isidore the Farmer

*I*sidore the Farmer was a simple worker in the fields near Madrid, Spain, at the end of the 11th century. He was very pious and prayed as he worked behind his plow. Soon, many miracles attached themselves to him. Once his master came to criticize him for going to Mass instead of working. The master expected to see the field empty but instead saw angels guiding the plow in Isidore's place.

Though poor, Isidore shared all he had with those who were even more needy. One day, after Isidore had given away his last bit of food, a beggar appeared at the door. Isidore opened his cupboard, and it was filled with food.

Isidore was also kind to animals. One snowy day on the way to the mill, he passed a flock of birds pecking for food on the frosty ground. He poured half his sack of corn on the ground for the birds. When he reached the mill, the bag was again full, and the milled corn yielded double the amount of flour.

Isidore married a woman as virtuous as he, Maria Torribia. Their baby boy fell into a well and drowned. Isidore and Maria prayed for a miracle. As they prayed, the water rose up from the well and brought the baby to them, alive and unhurt.

Another time the parish had a dinner. Isidore and Maria arrived with a group of beggars. This upset parishioners who warned there would not be enough food. Yet as everyone filled up their plates, more food appeared in the pantry until the hall was overflowing with food. The parishioners were amazed, but Isidore said, "There is always enough for the poor of Jesus."

The faith of Isidore and Maria produced other miracles well known in Spain. He is the patron saint of farm workers, and her relics have been used to bring rain in times of drought. Even today, miracles and cures are reported at his grave, in which his body has remained incorruptible.

*S*aint Dymphna, as you did not waver when forced to choose between right and wrong, please help me follow the path to Jesus and His mercy.

Saint Dymphna

Dymphna is the patron of those suffering from emotional and mental illnesses. She was the daughter of Damon, a chieftain in Ireland in the seventh century. When Dymphna was fourteen, her mother died. This sudden tragedy drove Damon to insanity. In his madness, he decided to marry his daughter.

Dymphna refused, but she could not convince her father to give up his sinful plan to marry her. With her confessor, St. Gerebernus, she fled from Ireland to the continent of Europe, settling near Gheel, a small village in Belgium. They lived as hermits, and Dymphna quickly became known for her devotion to the poor.

Damon and his warriors followed and finally found her as reputation of her kindness spread through the countryside. The king's soldiers killed the priest but were afraid to kill Dymphna. Damon demanded one last time that she marry him. When she said no, he cut her head off with his sword.

A shrine was built on the spot where she was buried. Many miracles have taken place there, and an asylum for the mentally ill was created nearby in the 13th century. It still exists today and helps patients live useful and normal lives in the homes of local residents.

In the United States, a shrine to Dymphna has been built at Massillon, Ohio. It is next to one of the most modern hospitals in the world for treatment of mental illness, the Massillon Psychiatric Center. A very popular nine days' novena to St. Dymphna is recited worldwide stressing the virtues of faith, hope, charity, prudence, justice, temperance, fortitude, chastity and perseverance.

*S*aint Eugene de Mazenod, your gentle nature brought peace to the afflicted. Help me spread the good news about Jesus wherever I go.

Saint Eugene de Mazenod *Feast Day: May 21*

*P*atron saint of dysfunctional families, Eugene de Mazenod was seven years old when the French Revolution erupted in 1789, spreading terror and death throughout the land. His family fled France, and Eugene did not return until he was twenty. He saw that many people had lost belief in God.

Eugene de Mazenod became a Catholic priest and set about rebuilding the Church in France. Though born of a wealthy family, he preached among the poorest of the poor and helped doctors and nurses in hospitals. He nearly died from typhus while working in a prison. He built churches, ordained many new priests and developed catechisms for young people.

Along with several other French priests, Eugene de Mazenod founded the Missionary Oblates of Mary Immaculate. Their task was to work for peace and justice and aid families in distress. Often they would travel on foot to the most remote parts of France to visit people in need. Said Eugene de Mazenod, "Their principal service in the Church is to proclaim Christ and his kingdom to the most abandoned."

The work of the order soon spread to other countries. In 1847, millions of people in Ireland were dying of famine. Eugene de Mazenod appealed to his parishioners for money to buy food for the Irish. Today, the Missionary Oblates of Mary Immaculate has 5,000 missionaries in sixty-eight countries.

Eugene de Mazenod was named Bishop of Marseille and served in that position until his death in 1861. "To love the Church," he said, "is to love Jesus Christ, and vice versa. Our mission is to proclaim the kingdom of God and seek it before all else. Together we await Christ's coming in the fullness of his justice so that God may be all in all."

*S*aint Joan of Arc, you followed God's instructions and saved an entire nation. Help me heed the plans God has in store for me.

Saint Joan of Arc Feast Day: May 30

*J*oan of Arc is the patron saint of France. She was born in 1412 in the village of Domremy, France. She received solid religious education from her parents. As a young girl, she was known for her piety and her kindness to the poor. Often, when playing in the fields with her friends, she would leave their games and go aside to pray.

Joan lived during a time of war and strife. France had been fighting England for nearly one hundred years. When Joan was thirteen, she began receiving visions of St. Margaret of Antioch, St. Catherine of Alexandria and St. Michael the Archangel. The saints told her that she had been chosen by God to lead France to victory.

For three years Joan was unable to believe this was her true task. But in 1428 her visions said she must find the true king of France and help him reclaim his throne. Armed only with her trust in God, Joan convinced the leader of the French army to give her command of his troops. Holding a banner that read "Jesus, Mary," she led the army to one victory after another. After the English were defeated, Charles VII became the King of France and Joan was hailed as the savior of France.

Some French leaders hated Joan, and she was betrayed and sold to the English. They tried her as a heretic and had her burned at the stake in 1431. "God willing," she said to the executioner preparing her death, "this evening I shall be with God in Paradise."

In just over one year, Joan of Arc had changed the course of European history, simply because she had listened to the Voice of God.

*S*aint Anthony, you are the finder of what is lost. Help me never lose my belief in the power of God's miracles.

Saint Anthony

A native of Lisbon, Portugal, Anthony was just a child when he decided to devote his life to serving God. At age fifteen he became an Augustinian brother and shortly after performed one of his first miracles, curing a man who was possessed by the devil.

Though he hoped to become a martyr for the Catholic faith, Anthony instead became one of the Church's greatest teachers. He went to Italy and met St. Francis, joining the Franciscan order of monks in 1221. Anthony's ability to speak with great passion about God attracted large crowds. When he spoke in Padua, the entire city assembled to hear him. He possessed a loud, clear voice, a friendly manner, powerful memory and distinguished learning. Like St. Francis, Anthony had a special reverence for God's works in nature. He once was seen standing on a river bank preaching to a school of fish, who appeared to be listening in rapture.

Anthony also performed many miracles. When he was preaching outdoors in a thunderstorm, not one person was touched by a drop of water. Another time, a group of heretics tried to kill Anthony and served him a meal of poisoned food. Anthony made the Sign of the Cross over the plate and ate the food without suffering any harm. In the town of Padua, a young man who had cut his foot off approached Anthony with the foot, and the saint rejoined the foot and leg.

Anthony was once preaching at the funeral of a money-lender who had spent his life obsessed with gaining riches. Anthony was asked if he thought the man was in heaven. He replied, "That rich man is dead and buried in hell, but go to his treasures and there you will find his heart." The people went to the money-lender's grave and there — among piles of gold and silver — found the man's warm, still-beating heart.

Anthony died at age thirty-six of illness. Today, he is known as the finder of lost articles and the patron saint of the poor.

*S*aint Thomas More, you put loyalty to God above all earthly kings. Help me to stand strong when my faith is tested.

Saint Thomas More Feast Day: June 22

*T*homas More was an English poet, writer and lawyer who held many political positions in the early 1500s. He was a fair governor and a friend to the poor. At the peak of his career, Thomas More was appointed Lord Chancellor of England by King Henry VIII. The lord chancellor was second in power only to the king.

Thomas More's dedication to serving God by serving the people of his kingdom began early. At age thirteen he was placed in the household of Cardinal Morton, who was then the Archbishop of Canterbury and Lord Chancellor of England. Thomas More received training in the law and also spent time writing plays and poetry to cheer his fellow students.

Thomas More started each day with prayer, Mass and spiritual reading, no matter what official duties he had to perform. Thomas More wrote many books, including *Utopia*, in which he theorized about the perfect world. He also kept many pets and enjoyed scientific inquiries into nature and the animal kingdom.

In 1501 Thomas More was elected a member of Parliament, the first of many important positions including Under-Sheriff of London, Ambassador to Flanders, High Steward of Cambridge University and in 1529, Lord Chancellor.

In 1532, King Henry VIII declared he wanted to divorce his queen. Thomas More warned that this was forbidden by the Church. Henry then declared himself head of his own church, the Church of England. Again, Thomas More did not agree. He resigned as Lord Chancellor and would not swear an Oath of Supremacy to the new church. Henry was furious and had Thomas More thrown into prison.

Three years later, Thomas More was beheaded because he would not betray his conscience and belief in the Supreme Power of God. Said Thomas More as he awaited his death, "I am the king's good servant, but God's first." He is the patron saint of statesmen and politicians.

*S*aint John the Baptist, you prepared the world for the coming of Jesus. Help me make my world a more welcome place for God's presence.

Saint John the Baptist

*T*he Archangel Gabriel appeared to Zachary and Elizabeth and said their unborn son was to be the Messenger of God. The child grew up to become John the Baptist, a prophet who preached that the Son of God was coming to Israel in the days at hand.

At the age of twenty-six, John the Baptist moved to the desert beyond the Jordan River and spent a long time praying and fasting, living off locusts and wild honey. Some thought John the Baptist was the Messiah, but he humbly insisted he was only a "Voice crying in the wilderness." As he roamed throughout Israel, he told all who would listen that they should repent because the true Messiah would soon arrive.

One day John was speaking to a crowd. A man he had never seen approached him and asked to be baptized. John knew that this was Jesus, the Messiah, and he said he was not worthy to baptize the Son of God. Yet, in obedience to the will of God, he finally baptized Jesus. A dove came down from the sky, and a voice from the sky declared, "Thou art My beloved Son, in Thee I am well pleased."

John the Baptist knew this was the sign of the Holy Spirit. "Behold the Lamb of God," he cried. "Behold Him who takes away the sin of the world."

John the Baptist continued to preach the message of repentance and encouraged his disciples to follow Jesus. Around 31 A.D. he was seized by King Herod and beheaded for his refusal to deny the divinity of Christ. John the Baptist is the patron saint of baptisms and converts.

*S*aint Peter, you were the rock upon which Jesus built His church. Help me be a person others can depend upon to be just and kind.

Saint Peter

*L*ike his brother Andrew, Peter was a fisherman in Galilee. His birth name was Simon, but when he joined the Apostles, Jesus gave him a new name — Peter, which means "the rock." Jesus intended that Peter take on the biggest role in building the new Church.

Peter became the leader of the Apostles. He was at Jesus' side at the Transfiguration, the raising of Jairus' daughter and the Agony of the Garden of Gethsemane. He helped organize the Last Supper and was the first person to see Christ after His Resurrection.

In declaring Peter to be head of the Catholic Church, Jesus said, "Upon this rock I will build My Church, and the gates of hell shall not prevail against it. To you I will give the keys of the kingdom of heaven. Whatever you bind on earth shall be bound also in heaven. Whatever you loose on earth shall be loosed also in heaven."

Peter was the first Apostle to perform a miracle in the name of Christ. When a crippled beggar asked for money, Peter told him he had none. "In the name of Jesus Christ of Nazareth, walk!" The beggar rose and walked, cured of his lameness.

Peter went to Rome and in the heart of the pagan Roman Empire established the Catholic Church. He converted many people there before being ordered to die upon the cross in 64 A.D. He asked to be crucified upside down because he believed himself unworthy to die in the same manner as Jesus.

*S*aint Paul, you had the courage to open your heart to the love of Christ. Help me to never close my mind to Jesus' words.

Paul was born in Tarsus, the son of a Jew of the tribe of Benjamin. His given name was Saul, and he was a Roman citizen educated in Jerusalem.

When the first Christians began preaching the words of Jesus, Saul hated them. He assisted at the stoning of St. Stephen, the leader of a colony of Greek Jews who had become Christians. One day, as he rode to Damascus to arrest another group of Christians, he was thrown to the ground by a lightning bolt. He heard a voice that said, "Why do you persecute Me?" "Who are You?" asked Saul. The voice replied, "I am Jesus, whom you are persecuting."

The accident blinded Saul, and he had to be led by hand to Damascus. There, he was baptized and instantly recovered his sight. He took on the Christian name Paul and became a missionary throughout the Middle East and the Mediterranean.

Besides talking to people about Jesus, Paul wrote letters, or "epistles," that were carried to the Christian communities. These epistles gave people hope and encouraged them to stay strong in their faith. Much of what Paul said in the epistles is used in our liturgy today.

"I remind you to stir into flame the gift of God that you have through the imposition of my hands," wrote Paul while he was in prison. "For God did not give us a spirit of cowardice but rather of power and love and self-control. So do not be ashamed of your testimony to our Lord, nor of me, a prisoner for His sake; but bear your share of the hardship for the gospel with the strength that comes from God."

After many years of missionary work, Paul reached Rome and met Peter, the Apostle who was now Pope. Like Peter, Paul was martyred in 64 A.D. Because these two saints were so important in shaping the early Church, they share the same feast day of June 29.

*S*aint Thomas, you overcame doubt to tell the world of God's mercy and power. Help me overcome any doubts I have about God's purpose for me.

Saint Thomas

*T*homas was one of twelve Apostles and had been a fisherman in Galilee. He was a simple man but faithful to Jesus.

At the Last Supper, Jesus said, "I go to prepare a place for you. And where I go you know, and the way you know." Thomas replied, "Lord, we know not where you go, and how can we know the way?" To this Jesus answered, "I am the way, the truth and the life."

Later that night, when Jesus told his Apostles he was going to leave them and would likely die, Thomas cried, "Let us also go, that we may die with Him."

Yet this saint is often called "Doubting Thomas." Thomas was so full of sorrow for Christ's death, that even after the Resurrection, he could not believe the Apostles who said they had seen Jesus risen from the dead. The Gospel of John reports Thomas stating, "Except I shall see in His hands the print of the nails, and put my finger into the place of the nails, and put my hand into His side, I will not believe."

Eight days after Easter, Jesus again came to see the Apostles, suddenly appearing in a closed room. This time Thomas was there, and he saw our Lord in all His resurrected glory. Jesus told Thomas to touch His hands and the wound in His side. "Do not be faithless but believing."

Overcome, Thomas fell down on his knees and shouted, "My Lord and my God!" Jesus replied, "Because you have seen Me, Thomas, you have believed. Blessed are those who have not seen and have believed."

Inspired by what was now an unshakable faith, Thomas traveled to Mesopotamia, Abyssinia and Persia where he preached the word of Christ for many years before being martyred in India. He is the patron saint against doubt.

*S*aint Maria Goretti, your faith in God was strong enough to make you prefer death to sin. Help me know what is right and give me the strength to do it.

Saint Maria Goretti Feast Day: July 6

*M*aria Goretti is the patron saint of youth and of parents whose children have died. Her story is at first a very sad story. In 1902, this innocent twelve-year-old Italian farm girl was attacked by a man named Allessandro Serenelli, who desired her to commit a sin of the flesh. Maria refused, saying she could not sin in such a manner.. Furious, Allessandro choked and stabbed her to death.

Before Maria died, she forgave her attacker and asked God to forgive him. She died holding a crucifix and medal of Our Lady. Allessandro was sentenced to thirty years in prison. He was defiant and did not ask forgiveness for his crime.

But the story does not end here. While in prison, Allessandro had a vision of Maria. He saw a garden where a young girl, dressed in white, gathered lilies. The girl smiled and offered him the lilies. As he took them, each lily transformed into a bright white flame. When he woke, Allessandro was truly sorry for his crime and at last repented. After his release from prison, he went straight to Maria's mother and begged her forgiveness, which she gave. Allessandro spent the rest of his life as a gardener in a monastery, devoting his life to God.

Because of the violence that ended her life as she defended her faith, Maria Goretti was declared a martyr. Because the purity of her soul continued to reach out into the world even after her death, Maria Goretti was declared a saint. The ceremony in Rome took place in 1950 and was attended by a quarter million people, including Maria Goretti's mother. This was the only time a parent has been present at her child's canonization.

*S*aint Benedict, you showed how a simple life can bring forth the miracles of heaven. Help me make time for God in my busy day.

Saint Benedict

*B*enedict was born of a noble Italian family in 480 A.D. His name in Latin means "blessed." Even as a boy, he was virtuous and eager to serve God. At age fourteen, he wished to no longer be distracted by the evils of the world, and he became a hermit. Benedict lived in a mountain cave outside Rome for three years until a priest found him and spread word of his holiness.

Benedict searched for a place to build a monastery. He chose a site that had been used as a pagan temple for many centuries. He destroyed the temple and consecrated the ground to Jesus Christ. Benedict's monastery still stands at the village of Monte Cassino, eighty miles southeast of Rome, where it was rededicated in 1964 by Pope Paul VI.

People came to Benedict for spiritual aid and to be inspired by his example of prayer. Benedict foretold many prophecies and performed many miracles. He once resurrected a boy from the dead by praying over his body. Another time, a monk lost the head of his axe in a river. Benedict told him to throw the handle in after it. The axe rose from the river to become one with the handle.

Under his direction, many monasteries were founded according to one simple rule: "Pray and work." Benedict believed that the everyday work done by monks was an expression of the richness in grace of their lives. Work is holy, idleness leads to sin.

Yet Benedict did not believe the purpose of a monastery was to provide escape from the world. Rather, he encouraged his followers to influence the world with good works that brought Jesus Christ into the lives of ordinary people. At one time, over 40,000 monasteries throughout the world followed the Benedictine Rule. Benedict died in 547 A.D. while praying.

Blessed Kateri Tekakwitha, your faith in God was as bold as that of any warrior. Help me find courage to follow the way of Christ.

Blessed Kateri Tekakwitha *Feast Day: July 14*

*K*ateri Tekakwitha was the daughter of a Mohawk warrior and an Algonquin mother. She grew up near Auriesville, New York, in the late1600s. Her Indian name means "she puts things in order," and at an early age Kateri decided to put God first in her life.

Kateri was four years old when her parents died of smallpox, a disease which also afflicted Kateri. She was adopted by her uncle and his wife. She was an obedient child and performed household duties as did other young Mohawk girls her age.

When Kateri was eleven, a group of French Jesuit missionaries visited her uncle, and she heard them talk about Jesus. She wanted to know more about a God who loved people instead of punishing them. When she was twenty, Kateri was baptized. She made her first Holy Communion on Christmas Day.

Kateri lived a life dedicated to prayer and providing care for the sick and aged. Kateri loved the rosary and sang her prayers in the Indian way, as she went around the beads. In church, people gathered near Kateri. They said they felt closer to God when she prayed.

It was hard for a woman to live in the wilderness without a husband. Though her people wished for her to marry, Kateri chose to stay a virgin and be the bride of Jesus.

Called "the lily of the Mohawk," Kateri died of illness in 1680 at age twenty-four. Along with St. Francis, she is a patron saint of the environment and ecology. There is a shrine to Kateri at Caughnawaga, Cananda. Caughnawaga means "laughing waters" in the Mohawk language, and the stream in which Kateri was baptized still flows.

*S*aint Mary Magdalen, you followed Jesus through good times and bad. Teach me to stay faithful to God's word all the days of my life.

Saint Mary Magdalen

Feast Day: July 22

*B*efore she met Jesus, Mary Magdalen was a notorious sinner and very proud. Yet, when Jesus passed through her district of Galilee, she renounced her way of life and became a devout follower of the Son of God.

Some time later, Jesus was at the home of a rich man. Mary Magdalen came to ask Jesus' forgiveness and wept over His feet. To show her sorrow and humility, she wiped them dry with her hair and then anointed them with expensive perfume and oil. Jesus was moved by her honesty and said, "Many sins are forgiven you, because you have loved very much."

After this meeting with Jesus, Mary Magdalen gave herself over entirely to the service of Christ. She became one of the holy women who followed Jesus in His travels in Galilee and finally to Jerusalem, where He would die for humankind's sins.

Mary Magdalen served Jesus and His Apostles even after the Crucifixion. She gave Jesus aid as he struggled to Calvary and remained at the foot of the cross, comforting Jesus as He died. Two days later, she went to Jesus' tomb and was the first person to whom the risen Christ revealed Himself. She announced His Resurrection to the apostles and for this reason is often called "the apostle to the apostles." Even after the Apostles came to the tomb and left, she stayed, longing to see Jesus once more.

Mary Magdalen is the patron saint of hairdressers and penitent sinners. Her feast day is July 22.

*S*aint Christopher, you were not afraid to take up the burden of Christ's work. Give me strength to carry my burdens each day without complaint or despair.

Saint Christopher Feast Day: July 25

*T*here are many legends about Christopher, who died as a martyr during the third century. His name in Greek means "Christ-bearer" or "one who carries Christ." Before his conversion to Christianity, he was called Offerus and was a ferryman in the province of Lycia. He was a giant of a man, and his job was to carry travelers across a river.

One stormy night Offerus stood on the river bank. A small child appeared and asked to be carried across, though the thunder and rain were beating down very hard. Offerus agreed and lifted the child on his shoulders. The weight of the child was enormously heavy. With each step, Offerus' burden became heavier. Half-way across the swollen river, he felt certain he would falter and he and his passenger would drown. Summoning his last ounce of strength, Offerus reached the opposite bank, where he realized the child was Christ. The heaviness he had felt was the weight of the Son of God carrying all the sins of the world.

The Christ Child gave Offerus his new name of Christopher. He asked Christopher to plant his staff in the ground. Christopher did so, and a beautiful tree sprang up immediately. Christopher began to preach the Christian faith to everyone he met. His zeal soon attracted the ill will of the authorities, and he was put to death.

Christopher is the patron saint of travelers, especially those driving in automobiles. You may also pray to him for help in storms or plagues.

*S*aint Joachim, your devotion to God brought you the divine gift of fatherhood. Help me prepare to serve God when I grow up.

Saint Joachim

*J*oachim was the father of the Blessed Virgin Mary. In Hebrew, the name Joachim means "Yahweh prepares" — a sign that Joachim would play an important role in bringing the Son of God, or Yahweh, into the world.

For many years Joachim and his wife, Anne, had no children, and they were very sad. On a feast day Joachim went to the temple to offer a sacrifice. He was told that men without children could not enter the temple on this day.

Joachim was very saddened and did not return home. Instead, he went to the mountains and prayed to God for a child. One day when Joachim was alone in the fields, the Angel Gabriel came and stood before him. "I am the Angel of the Lord," said the Holy Messenger, "and it is God Himself who sends me. He has heard your prayers. Anne, your spouse, will bear a daughter whose happiness will be above that of other women; She will be blessed and named the Mother of eternal blessing."

Not only had God answered Joachim's prayer, but Joachim was given the honor and responsibility of raising a child who would become the Mother of God. St. John Damascene once said, "Joachim and Anne, how blessed a couple! All creation is indebted to you. For at your hands the Creator was offered a gift excelling all other gifts: a chaste mother, who alone was worthy of Him."

The story of Joachim and Anne shows that, even though we may not know when or in what way, we are each chosen by God for a divine purpose in this world.

Joachim shares a feast day with his wife, St. Anne, on July 26. He is the patron saint of fathers and grandfathers.

*S*aint Anne, as you never lost hope in the power of God, help me
believe in the power of prayer to work miracles in this life.

Saint Anne *Feast Day: July 26*

*F*or many years Anne of Nazareth and her husband Joachim were childless. But they prayed often and sincerely that God would grant them a child. They promised to dedicate their child to the service of God.

One day, an angel appeared and told them they would have a child. "Anne, the Lord has looked upon thy tears," said the angel. "Thou shalt conceive and give birth, and the fruit of thy womb shall be blessed by all the world." The child who was born was Mary, the Mother of Jesus.

Of course, neither Anne nor Joachim knew their daughter would someday give birth to the Messiah. They simply did their duty as good parents, raising Mary to be a virtuous and kind woman — a woman who would herself accept a call from heaven to do God's will upon earth. For this reason, Anne is the patron saint of mothers and of women in childbirth.

After Anne died, many legends sprang up about her holy relics. Some are believed to have resided in Constantinople and in the Provencal and Breton areas of France. Some legends even state she lived in Brittany, and she is very popular there yet today.

The Canadian village of Sainte-Anne-de-Beaupré, settled by French colonists who came to Quebec in the 17th century, has a shrine to Anne that is known worldwide. In 1658 a ship sailing up the St. Lawrence River was about to be sunk in a terrible storm. The sailors prayed to Anne, and the storm ceased immediately. Since then, numerous miracles have taken place there. Each year more than a million pilgrims visit the shrine to Anne, the faith-filled and patient mother of the Virgin Mary and grandmother of Jesus.

*S*aint Martha, your belief in God's power brought a miracle. Help me use my faith in Jesus to make miracles for others.

Saint Martha

*M*artha was the sister of Mary and Lazarus of Bethany, a small village near Jerusalem. Jesus came often to the family's home as He traveled through Israel. Martha always offered Jesus and His disciples food and shelter.

One day Lazarus became very sick, and Martha was heartbroken. She heard Jesus was preaching nearby. Right away Martha went to Jesus and said, "Lord, the one you love is ill."

Jesus told her not to worry, "This illness is not unto death. It is for the glory of God, so that the Son of God may be glorified by means of it."

Martha was confused, but Jesus' words gave her hope. Yet when she returned home, Lazarus had died. As the elder sister, Martha took charge of the funeral. Four days later, when Lazarus had already been put in the tomb, Martha met Jesus on the road. She told Him, "Lord, if You had been here, my brother would not have died." Yet her faith in Jesus as a healer was still strong. "Even now I know that whatever You ask from God, God will give You."

Jesus told her that Lazarus would rise from the dead. "I am the resurrection and the Life," He told her. "Whoever believes in Me, even if he dies, will live, and everyone who lives and believes in Me will never die." He asked Martha if she believed this. She said, "Yes, Lord, I believe that You are the Christ, the Son of God, who has come into the world."

By now, many people had gathered and they found it hard to believe what Jesus was saying. Jesus led them to where Lazarus was buried. He ordered the stone over the tomb rolled back. In a loud voice He called, "Lazarus, come forth!"

The man who everyone believed had been dead walked out of the tomb, alive and a testament to the power of God. By showing her faith and courage, Martha obtained a miracle. She is the patron saint of servants and cooks.

$\mathcal{S}$aint Ignatius Loyola, you used your strength to combat the foes of the Church and enlighten her enemies. In some small way, help me spread knowledge about Jesus each day.

Saint Ignatius Loyola *Feast Day: July 31*

*P*atron of soldiers, Ignatius served in the royal Spanish army during the early 1500s. He was wounded in battle and not expected to live. At the door of death, Ignatius dreamed St. Peter touched him and healed his wounds. When he woke, Ignatius was healed.

Impressed by this miracle, Ignatius read books on the life of Christ and the lives of the saints. He was inspired by these stories and began to think, "What if I should do what St. Francis or St. Dominic did?"

Ignatius left the hospital but did not return to the army. Instead, he gave up his life as a soldier for the King of Spain to become a soldier for Jesus Christ. In 1534, Ignatius founded the Society of Jesus, a religious order devoted to the service of the Church and the salvation of souls. The Jesuits, as the members of the Society of Jesus are called, soon spread the teachings of Ignatius around the world. Today, there are more than 500 Jesuit universities and colleges that teach over 200,000 students a year.

St. Ignatius gave his followers practical advice. He wrote, "Do not let any occasion of gaining merit pass without taking care to draw some spiritual profit from it; as, for example, from a sharp word which someone may say to you; from an act of obedience imposed against your will; from an opportunity which may occur to humble yourself, or to practice charity, sweetness and patience. All of these occasions are gain for you, and you should seek to procure them; and at the close of that day, when the greatest number of them have come to you, you should go to rest most cheerful and pleased, as the merchant does on the day when he had had most chance for making money, for on that day business has prospered with him."

*S*aint Dominic, you defended the faith against lies and *falsehood. Help me see the truth of God's way.*

Saint Dominic *Feast Day: August 8*

Dominic was born in Spain in 1170 of wealthy parents, and his destiny to serve God was apparent even before he was born. While he was still in the womb, his mother had a vision of her son as a dog that would set the world on fire with a torch it carried in its mouth. When Dominic was baptized, his mother saw a bright star shining from his chest. These visions convinced her that Dominic would do great things.

At an early age Dominic himself heard God calling him to serve humankind. During a famine he sold his school books to feed the poor. Another time, he offered to exchange himself to free a slave.

Dominic became a priest and founded the Order of Friars Preachers, a religious order that became known as the Dominicans in tribute to his leadership. One night, Dominic had a dream of a beggar who would do great things for the Church. The next day, Dominic met a beggar in the street. He said, "You are my companion and must walk with me. If we hold together, no earthly power can withstand us." The beggar was none other than St. Francis of Assisi.

Dominic traveled throughout Spain and France, preaching the word of God and fighting against heretics. Dominic often became discouraged at the success of his mission and suffered much doubt. One day he received a vision from the Blessed Virgin who showed him a wreath of roses. She told him to say the rosary daily and teach it to all who would listen. Soon after, Dominic converted the heretics.

Dominic was twice chosen to be a bishop. He refused because it would keep him from living the simple life of his fellow monks. Dominic died in 1221 and is the patron saint of scientists.

*S*aint Clare, you spread the word of God through good works. Help me show the face of Jesus' kindness to everyone I meet.

Clare was the daughter of an Italian count and countess. After hearing St. Francis of Assisi preach in the streets, she decided to give up her life of privilege and devote her life to God.

Clare founded a religious order, the Order of Poor Ladies (Poor Clares), that was based on the Franciscan Order of St. Francis. The Poor Clares traveled throughout Europe leading lives of work and prayer, penance and contemplation, as they helped the Franciscan brothers in their mission to the poor. Clare and her sisters wore no shoes, ate no meat, lived in a simple home and stayed silent most of the time. Yet they were very happy.

The power of Clare's piety was made clear even before she died. The army of Frederick II came to attack her convent after looting the entire countryside nearby. Clare stood before the front gate facing the enemy. She knelt and held the Blessed Sacrament, praying, "Deliver not to beasts, O Lord, the souls of those who confess Your Name!" A voice from the Host replied, "My protection will never fail you." The attacking army was seized with terror and fled, sparing the convent.

Clare was also concerned about the welfare of her fellow nuns. Often, she would get up late at night to tuck in her sisters who had kicked off their bed covers. She daily meditated on the Passion. "Christ is the splendor of eternal glory," she said, "the brightness of eternal light, and the mirror without cloud."

Toward the end of her life, when Clare was too ill to attend Mass, an image of the service would display itself on the wall of her room. For this reason, Clare is the patron saint of television.

*S*aint Maximilian Kolbe, you never stopped trying to teach the goodness of Christ, even unto your last breath. Show me how to use love to overcome evil.

Saint Maximilian Kolbe Feast Day: August 14

*P*atron saint of journalists and political prisoners, Maximilian Kolbe was a Franciscan priest born in Poland in 1894. As a youth, he was mischievous, and his mother often worried about what he would grow up to be. After praying before a statue of the Blessed Mother, Maximilian told his mother he had seen Mary and that she had shown him two crowns, a white and a red. The white crown represented purity, the red represented martyrdom. The Blessed Virgin asked which crown he would take. Maximilian asked for both.

Maximilian founded the Immaculata Movement that encouraged devotion to Mary. This movement spread around the world, and Maximilian went to Japan and India to build monasteries for the Immaculata Movement. He started Catholic magazines and newspapers to tell the truth about evil things many politicians were doing in the world.

When World War II began, Maximilian was in Nazi Germany. He was thrown into prison for speaking out against the war. One day, he was beaten and left for dead. The prisoners sneaked him into the camp hospital where he spent his time recovering and hearing confessions. When he returned to the camp, Maximilian ministered to other prisoners, conducting Mass and delivering communion using smuggled bread and wine.

Not long after, a prisoner escaped, and the prison guards decided that ten men must die. Maximilian offered his life in place of a young man who was a husband and father. The guards accepted Maximilian's offer, and he died of starvation in 1941.

He told the other prisoners before he died, "Courage, my sons, Don't you see that we are leaving on a mission? They pay our fare in the bargain. What a piece of good luck! The thing to do now is to pray well in order to win as many souls as possible."

*S*aint Rose of Lima, your humility was a great example to many. Help me learn that my value lies not in the eyes of others but in how well I serve God.

Saint Rose of Lima *Feast Day: August 23*

*R*ose is the first native of the New World to be made a saint. Born of Spanish parents in Lima, Peru, in 1586, Rose promised her life to God while still a child. A few years later, Rose became a Dominican nun and worked in the convent garden, raising vegetables and making embroidered items to help the poor. She spent almost every moment of her life from that day forth praying for the conversion of sinners. She is considered to be the founder of social services in the Americas.

Rose's prayers were said to be very powerful. When a fleet from Holland prepared to attack the city of Lima, Rose knelt before the tabernacle and prayed for the city to be saved. Shortly after, the fleet sailed away without firing a shot.

Rose wrote, "Apart from the cross there is no other ladder by which we may get to heaven. If only mortals would learn how great it is to possess divine grace, how beautiful, how noble, how precious. How many riches it hides within itself, how many joys and delights! No one would complain about his cross or about troubles that may happen to him, if he would come to know the scales on which they are weighed when they are distributed to men."

Rose died in 1617 and is the patron saint of Latin America and the Philippines, as well as gardeners and florists. Her shrine, located in downtown Lima, is visited continuously by pilgrims in search of a miracle. On August 23, her feast day, pilgrims cast letters describing their needs into a wishing well or visit the hermitage Rose herself built.

$\mathcal{S}$aint Monica, you showed how powerful prayer can be. Help me be patient in my prayers, secure in the knowledge that God's will is being done.

Saint Monica Feast Day: August 27

*M*onica was born to Christian parents in the fourth century. She was given in marriage to a pagan husband, who was often unkind to her. For many years Monica served her husband with humility and prayed for him to accept Christianity. On his deathbed, he finally asked to be baptized and enjoy the grace of God.

Monica had an even more difficult time trying to bring her son Augustine to God. Monica prayed often and with persistence but with little apparent success. Several priests even said his conversion would not be possible and that Augustine's soul was too far from God. Replied Monica, "Nothing is far from God."

One day Monica had a vision where she seemed to be standing on a wooden beam suspended in mid-air surrounded by a bright light. She was lamenting over her son's absence. A voice asked her why she was crying. She answered and the voice told her to stop crying. She saw Augustine standing next to her and was comforted. She repeated the vision to her son, and he responded that they might easily be together if Monica renounced her Christian faith. "No," she replied. "The voice did not say I was with you. It said that you were with me."

Monica never stopped praying. She followed Augustine to Rome and then to Milan, always trying to convince him to see the error of his ways. Monica also performed many charitable works for the poor and joined a convent to strengthen her own faith while seeking to convert her son.

She also received the counsel of St. Ambrose, who was able to win Augustine's heart to Christ. Augustine became a bishop and a saint. Monica had prayed for his conversion for seventeen years, saying "it is not possible that the son of so many tears should perish."

Monica died in 387 A.D. She is the patron saint of married women.

*S*aint Augustine, you never stopped searching for the path to God. Help me find my way to Jesus's light through the darkness of temptation.

Saint Augustine

Augustine was born in Africa in the fourth century. His mother was St. Monica, but as a youth Augustine had no interest in God and lived a sinful life.

One day, he heard a child singing, "Take up and read!" Augustine picked up the nearest book. It was the Letters of St. Paul, and the first passage he saw told him to put away all impurity and to live according to Jesus.

From that moment, Augustine started life anew. He became a priest, a bishop and a famous Catholic writer who worked hard to correct errors in belief that were rising as the Church grew. He encouraged charity to the poor and once said, "God has no need of your money, but the poor have. You give it to the poor, and God receives it."

Even today, Augustine's writings contain much wisdom about our daily lives. "God bestows more consideration on the purity of the intention with which our actions are performed than on the actions themselves," he said. "The honors of this world, what are they but puff, and emptiness and peril of falling? The love of worldly possessions is a sort of bird line, which entangles the soul, and prevents it flying to God. What do you possess if you possess not God?"

Augustine is a patron saint for those who struggle with trying to break a bad habit. As he wrote, "Our hearts were made for You, O Lord, and they are restless until they rest in You. God does not command impossibilities, but by commanding admonishes you do what you can and to pray for what you cannot, and aids you that you may be able. Conquer yourself and the world lies at your feet."

*S*aint Raymond, your love for your fellow man overcame all earthly powers. Remind me to turn to God when I am in need.

Saint Raymond Feast Day: August 31

*R*aymond's life began with a miracle. He was taken from the womb of his mother after she died in childbirth. As a child in Spain, he preferred to read religious books above all others. Soon, he expressed the desire to enter religious life, but his father ordered him to manage the family farm and become a wealthy businessman. Raymond willingly performed his work, but he was not interested in pursuing riches. Instead, he spent his time with the workers, praying and studying until his father finally allowed him to become a priest.

Raymond joined the Order of Our Lady of Mercy or the Mercaderians in Barcelona. In the 13th century, Spain was at war with Muslim nations of North Africa. The Mercaderian Order was dedicated to ransoming Christian captives taken prisoner by the Muslims and held as slaves.

With uncommon bravery, Raymond devoted his entire fortune to this cause. When he ran out of money, he gave himself up as a captive to free another prisoner. In prison, he converted some of his guards. This angered the warden who drilled a hole through his lips with a hot iron and attached a padlock to keep him from preaching about Jesus.

Still, this did not stop Raymond from his mission. After several years, he was freed and returned to Spain, where he continued to raise money to free slaves. Pope Gregory IX appointed him a Cardinal, but Raymond continued to live as a poor monk.

Raymond died of a fever while on a journey to Rome to visit the Pope. He is the patron saint of women in labor and of persons falsely accused.

$\mathcal{B}$lessed Mother Teresa, your works of Christian kindness inspired millions of people and helped bring us a step closer to the Paradise envisioned by God for his children. Help me learn ways in which I can help others feel the joy of God on Earth.

Blessed Mother Teresa of Calcutta *Feast Day: September 5*

*T*eresa of Calcutta is best known as Blessed Mother Teresa, in recognition of the tender care she gave to the poorest of the poor. She was born in 1910 of Albanian parents in Macedonia and her name was Agnes. When she entered the Order of the Sisters of Our Lady of Loreto at age 18, she took the name Teresa from the French nun, St. Thérèse of Lisieux.

Mother Teresa first went to India in 1928. While teaching at a school for wealthy children in Calcutta, she was astonished and saddened by the extreme poverty and suffering of the thousands of less fortunate people who lived and died on the city's streets. In 1948, she was allowed to leave her job at the school to start a ministry among the poor, the Missionaries of Charity.

Mother Teresa believed the poor were the image of Christ on earth, and the Missionaries of Charity were required to take a special vow of service to the poor. She taught the children of the slums how to read and write by writing in the dirt. She saw that even one person could do much to make a difference in the lives of many.

Mother Teresa's example was followed by many people, and the Missionaries of Charity took their mission to the people of five continents and 30 countries where they have founded homes for the dying, refuges for the care and teaching of orphans and abandoned children, treatment centers and hospitals for those suffering from leprosy, centers and refuges for alcoholics, the aged and street people. In 1979, she was awarded the Nobel Peace Prize for her lifetime work of serving her fellow children of God.

Mother Teresa spoke often of the importance of prayer. She said, "Feel often during the day the need for prayer and pray. Prayer opens the heart, till it is capable of containing God himself. Ask and seek and your heart will be big enough to receive Him and keep Him as your own."

Mother Teresa died in 1997 and was beatified on October 19, 2003 by Pope John Paul II.

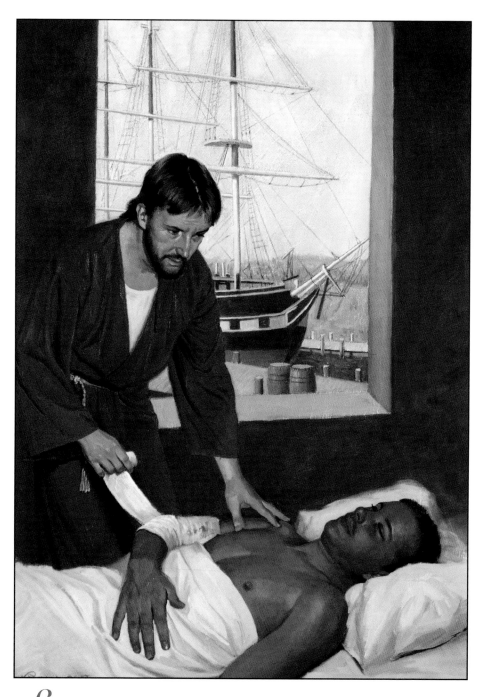

*S*aint Peter Claver, your love for God's children knew no boundaries. Help me show compassion to the victims of social injustice.

Saint Peter Claver

Peter Claver spent forty-four years caring for the most persecuted people of his day — African slaves in the Spanish colonies of the New World.

The son of a Catalonian farmer, Peter Claver was born in 1581. He earned his first degrees at the University of Barcelona. At the age of twenty he became a Jesuit priest. In 1610 he left Spain for the port city of Cartagena, South America. His special mission was to tell the African slaves about Jesus Christ and His love and mercy.

This was no easy task, since the slaves were given little love or mercy from their cruel colonial masters. Peter Claver worked to have slavery abolished and demanded the slaves be treated decently. He boarded the slave ships that entered the harbor and took food, drink and medicine to the slaves, many of whom were near death after their terrible ordeal. He instructed them about Jesus and the eternal life without toil that awaited them in heaven. Said Peter Claver, "We must speak with our hands by giving, before we try to speak to them with our lips." He converted more than 300,000 slaves to Christ.

Peter Claver continued to bring the light of the Church to his converts even after they left the slave ships. He followed them to the plantations to which they were sent, encouraged them to live as Christians, and prevailed on their masters to treat them humanely.

Many miracles took place during Peter Claver's life. He brought a dead girl back to life by sprinkling her with holy water. He often used his long cloak to comfort the ill and protect them from exposure. Soon, people began to touch his cloak and be healed of sickness.

Peter Claver also organized charitable societies among the Spanish colonists similar to those organized in Europe by St. Vincent de Paul. He died in 1654 and is the patron saint of African missions and inter-racial justice.

*S*aint Robert Bellarmine, you devoted your life to imparting God's wisdom. Help me keep my mind open to the truth of heaven.

Saint Robert Bellarmine *Feast Day: September 17*

*R*obert Bellarmine was born in 1542 in Italy, the third of ten children. He was infused with a great desire for learning at an early age. As a boy, he often spent his time repeating the sermons he heard to his brothers and sisters. He also enjoyed explaining catechism lessons to neighborhood children.

Robert Bellarmine joined the Society of Jesus at age eighteen and taught Greek, Hebrew and theology at Louvain University. He wrote many books and spoke out against the heresies of the day that were causing disbelief and even war throughout Europe. He believed very deeply in education for all people and taught catechism to children whenever he could.

Robert Bellarmine was an open-minded scholar who promoted knowledge as the best way to find God. He defended Galileo for his unpopular views on science. He also taught that the authority of kings to rule is given from God to the people, who should give power only to rulers who are morally fit.

Robert Bellarmine was the head of the Vatican library. In 1598 he was made a Cardinal by Pope Clement VIII and some years later was himself nominated to be Pope. Yet he refused to live in luxury and gave all his money to the poor. One time, he sold his expensive tapestries to clothe the poor. After all, he said, "the walls won't catch cold." Later he wrote, "Charity is that with which no man is lost, and without which no man is saved."

Robert Bellarmine died in 1621 and has been declared a Doctor of the Church. He is the patron saint of church lawyers and catechists.

$\mathcal{S}$aint Padre Pio, you showed us the love God has for his suffering people. Help me learn from your patient example that eternal blessings may often grow from temporary suffering.

Saint Padre Pio

Saint Pio was born Francesco Forgione in 1887 at Pietrelcina, Italy. When he was just five years old, he began to see heavenly visions and decided he would devote his life to serving God. At age 15, he entered the novitiate of the Capuchin Friars and was ordained a priest at age 22.

A month after he became a priest, Padre Pio was visited by Jesus and Mary. It was at this time he was given the Stigmata, the wounds of Christ. At first Padre Pio asked God to take away this gift because he feared people would believe he was only drawing attention to himself. But the Stigmata would stay with Padre Pio the rest of his life, reminding the world of Christ's Passion and victory over sin and death.

Padre Pio lived during the time of two of the worst wars in history, a time when millions of people died. He started prayer groups to pray for peace. These groups continue today with over 400,000 members worldwide. In 1956, Padre Pio founded the Home for the Relief of Suffering, a teaching hospital that serves 60,000 people a year and offers instruction in Christian medical practice.

Padre Pio believed there were five rules for spiritual growth: weekly confession, daily communion, spiritual reading, meditation and examination of conscience. He said, "Every Holy Mass, heard with devotion, produces in our souls marvelous effects, abundant spiritual and material graces which we, ourselves, do not know. It is easier for the earth to exist without the sun than without the Holy Sacrifice of the Mass!"

Padre Pio died in 1968, just a few hours after saying his final Mass. He was canonized on June 16, 2002 by Pope John Paul II.

*S*aint Vincent de Paul, as you saw the image of God in every person you met, teach me to love my neighbor with the same love I show Jesus.

Saint Vincent de Paul *Feast Day: September 27*

When Vincent de Paul was a boy in France during the 1580s, he had already embarked on a lifetime of good works. Coming back from the mill with flour for his family, if he met a poor man coming home, Vincent de Paul would give handfuls of his own flour.

Vincent de Paul became a priest but was captured by pirates and sold as a slave in Tunisia. He converted his captor and helped him escape to France. Vincent de Paul was especially concerned for the welfare of children. Each night, he walked through the streets of Paris rescuing infants and children left to die. Once he was seized by robbers who thought he carried a treasure. When Vincent de Paul opened his cloak, they saw an abandoned baby. "This is my treasure!" said Vincent de Paul. Shamed, they fell at his feet and joined him in prayer.

Vincent de Paul founded the Lazarist Fathers and the Daughters of Charity to continue his mission of helping the poor and the sick. He opened hospitals and homes for orphans and old people. He wrote, "It is our duty to prefer the service of the poor to everything else and to offer such service as quickly as possible. If a needy person requires medicine or other help during prayer time, do whatever has to be done with peace of mind. Offer the deed to God as your prayer. Charity is certainly greater than any rule. Moreover, all rules must lead to charity."

Vincent de Paul died in 1660 and is the patron saint of hospital and charity workers. To further his work in modern times, the St. Vincent de Paul Society was begun in Paris in 1833 by Frederic Ozanam. It has one million members worldwide in 130 countries and gives moral and material aid to the poor of all faiths.

$\mathcal{S}$aint Michael Archangel, you have protected humankind since the dawn of time. Guide my steps so they lead directly to God.

Saint Michael Archangel Feast Day: September 29

The Hebrew word for angel is "malach," which means "messenger." Angels like Michael are among the instruments by which God communicates divine will to humans.

Angels serve humans, too, in many ways. Angels have appeared on earth as guardians, guides, counselors, judges, matchmakers and interpreters. They have helped find lost articles, increase wealth, strengthen faith, calm storms, convert heathens, carry saints to heaven and turn the tide of battle to destroy God's enemies.

Michael is one of three archangels who reside closest to God. His name in Hebrew means "he who is like God." Michael was a leader in the heavenly battle against angels who rejected God to follow the evil angel Lucifer. Michael and the loyal angels overcame Lucifer and his followers and cast them out of heaven. Because of this, Michael has been called upon as a patron and protector from the time of the Apostles.

Among Michael's chief duties are these four: (1) to fight against Satan (2) to rescue the souls of the faithful from the power of the enemy, especially at the hour of death (3) to be the champion of God's people, the Jews in the Old Law, Christians in the New Testament (4) to call away human souls from earth and bring them to judgment. One of the most dramatic appearances of Michael on earth was when he told Abraham that he need not sacrifice his son Isaac to please God.

Although he is always called "the Archangel," many Church leaders place him over all the angels with the title "Prince of the Seraphim." Michael is the patron saint of grocers, mariners, paratroopers, police and those suffering from sickness.

*S*aint Raphael Archangel, you know the true beauty and goodness of heaven. Guide and protect me as I seek the way to Paradise.

Saint Raphael Archangel *Feast Day: September 29*

*R*aphael's name means "the healing of God." Along with Michael, he is one of three archangels who reside closest to God.

In the Old Testament, Raphael travelled with Tobias and guarded him on a dangerous journey to collect a debt for his family. Raphael protected Tobias from demons and wild beasts. When a giant fish attacked Tobias on the shores of the Tigris River, Raphael helped him tame it and then make medicine and food from the fish. All the time, Tobias did not know Raphael was an angel but thought he was simply a good friend.

Raphael and Tobias arrived at their destination safely and Tobias became engaged to marry a woman named Sara. Sara had been engaged before seven times, and each man had died just before the wedding. Raphael told Tobias not to fear but to pray with Sara for three nights. They did as Raphael said, and they were married without harm. When Tobias returned safely home, Raphael cured Tobias' father of blindness by telling Tobias to use the gall of the giant fish they had killed earlier in their journey.

At other times, Raphael is said to have appeared on earth to heal the wound on Jacob's leg and to give Noah a book of cures for humankind after the Great Flood. In the New Testament, Raphael is the angel who stirred the healing water in the pool of Bethsaida.

Like other good angels God has placed in service for His people, Raphael is a powerful ally. Raphael is the patron saint of travellers, good health and the blind. He is also known as the Angel of Love and the Angel of Joy. Raphael and Michael Archangel share the same feast day, September 29.

*S*aint Therese, you took delight in seeing God in the smallest of details. Help me see God's presence in my everyday tasks.

Saint Therese, the Little Flower   *Feast Day: October 1*

*T*herese Martin grew up in France in the 1870s. She was the youngest of ten children. She was a quiet girl and helpful around the busy household. But Therese had a secret wish. She felt sure that Jesus wanted her to spend her life loving him.

When she was only ten years old, Therese became very ill with fever. One night in her bedroom, she prayed for healing to a statue of the Virgin Mary. She saw the Virgin smile at her! The fever left instantly, and from that day on, Therese knew the power of prayer.

Therese joined the convent at fifteen and became a Carmelite nun in the town of Lisieux. She said her mission was to make God loved on earth. Therese found ways to live a simple life and become a Little Flower of Jesus. She kept a journal in which she wrote about the power of prayer and about finding heaven's beauty in the simple things around us. After she died, the journal was published as a book called *The Story of a Soul.* It has inspired millions of readers to seek God through prayer.

Though she was still very young, Therese became sick with tuberculosis, and her lungs began to fail. She would hide her pain with a smile. As she lay dying, she told her friends and family: "Pray to me, and I will answer you with a shower of roses." Many people believe after you pray to St. Therese and you hear the word "rose" or see or smell roses, she has heard your prayer and is working her miracle in heaven.

The feast day of St. Therese is October 1. She is the patron saint of airplane crews and pilots, those who suffer from illness and — most of all — those who grow flowers.

*S*aint Francis, you treated everyone as a divine child of God.
Help me see the presence of God in everyone I meet.

Saint Francis *Feast Day: October 4*

Francis was a wealthy young man in the Italian town of Assisi. No one loved gaiety and pleasure more than he. Francis took great delight in fine clothes and lively frolics and even fought frequent battles as a soldier in the local militia.

Despite his youthful sprees and carefree behavior, Francis still felt much sympathy for the poor. Even in the midst of his lavish spending on parties, he often gave money to the needy and to charity. He made a pilgrimage to Rome and visited the tomb of St. Peter. He saw that hardly any pilgrims had left money at the shrine. Francis offered his entire purse of gold and then exchanged his clothes with those of a tattered beggar. Francis stood for the rest of the day fasting among the swarm of beggars in front of the tomb.

A short time later, Francis was praying and gazing at Christ on the crucifix. The figure spoke to Francis and said, "Francis, rebuild My church." Francis believed it was God Himself who spoke to him. He sold all his belongings and rebuilt his local church with his own hands.

Francis soon realized that his call was not just to rebuild one church but to rebuild the entire Catholic Church on a foundation of merciful works. He believed this could be done by following the Gospel and by showing honor, respect and love to every person he met, be they beggar or king.

Francis started the order of Franciscan brothers and nuns to carry on his mission of helping the poor. In the year 1221 Francis encouraged people in the town of Greccio to erect a living monument to the birth of Jesus. This became the Christmas creche that is celebrated around the world.

A legend says that Francis was able to talk to animals and be understood by them. Francis is the patron saint of ecologists and of Catholic action.

*S*aint Teresa of Avila, you walked with Jesus every day of your life. Help me stay close to His side as I pass through the world.

Saint Teresa of Avila
Feast Day: October 15

*T*eresa of Avila was born of noble Spanish parents in 1515. As a child, she was crippled by illness. Prayers to St. Joseph cured her. Her mother died when Teresa was twelve, so Teresa turned in prayer to the Blessed Virgin Mary and asked if she would be her new mother.

At age seventeen, Teresa became a Carmelite nun and devoted the rest of her life to God's work on earth. She said, "Whenever we think of Christ we should recall the love that led Him to bestow on us so many graces and favors, and also the great love God showed in giving us in Christ a pledge of His love. For love calls for love in return."

She wrote several books about the Catholic faith and received many visions. She was instructed to reform the Carmelite Order, and she founded over thirty new convents and monasteries. Teresa believed very much in the importance of prayer and meditation to keep one's soul on the path to God. The new Order she founded was devoted to living a simple life of poverty nourished by prayer.

Yet, Teresa was always very humble. When she was made abbess of her convent, she put a statue of Our Lady in the seat she would ordinarily have occupied, to show who was the true leader of the community.

She wrote, "We need no wings to go in search of God, but have only to look upon Him present within us. Unlike our friends in the world, He will never abandon us when we are troubled or distressed. Blessed is the one who truly loves Him and always keeps Him near." Teresa of Avila died in 1582 and is the patron saint of people in need of grace. Because of her great writings, she has been named a Doctor of the Church.

$\mathcal{S}$aint Margaret Mary Alacoque, your love of God gave the world the vision of the Sacred Heart. Help me know the power of this holy devotion.

Saint Margaret Mary Alacoque

*M*argaret Mary Alacoque was born in France in 1647 and educated by the Poor Clares. She was sick in bed for five years with a crippling disease until healed by a vision of the Blessed Virgin. This healing convinced her to offer her life to God, and she became a Visitation nun.

One day, Margaret Mary Alacoque received a special vision of Jesus. He said, "Through you, My divine Heart wishes to spread its love everywhere on earth." Jesus instructed her to maintain a special devotion to His Sacred Heart. To those who followed these instructions, Jesus gave Twelve Promises of His blessing, mercy, consolation and guidance into eternal life with Him in heaven.

The Promises include all the graces necessary for a pure state of life, peace in the family, consolation in all troubles, a refuge during life and at the hour of death, abundant blessings on all undertakings, infinite mercy for sinners. The most important promise was the last: final repentance for those who shall receive Communion on the First Friday of nine consecutive months. "They shall not die under My displeasure," said Jesus to Margaret Mary Alacoque, "nor without receiving their Sacraments; my heart shall be their assured refuge at that last hour. "

Slowly, the news of this vision spread across Europe. It is now one of the most popular devotions in the Catholic Church. Wrote Margaret Mary Alacoque, "The Sacred Heart of Christ is an inexhaustible fountain, and its sole desire is to pour itself out into the hearts of the humble so as to free them and prepare them to lead lives according to His good pleasure."

Margaret Mary Alacoque died in 1690 and is the patron saint against polio.

*S*aint Gerard Majella, your kindness and love of Christ made the world a better place for children to be born. Help me live a life that is useful to others, especially the young.

Saint Gerard

Gerard Majella was born in Italy in 1726 and was twelve years old when his father died. He became an apprentice to a tailor and started his own tailoring business at age 19. He did not make much money at this work, however. What he did make, he ended up giving away to his family and then to the poor. At the age of 21 during the middle of Lent, Gerard Majella decided to be as completely like Christ as it was possible to be.

He joined the Redemptorist order of monks and worked very hard, serving his community as a gardener, sacristan, porter, cook, carpenter, clerk and, of course, tailor. Because of his great piety, wisdom and patience, Gerard Majella was permitted to counsel communities of religious women and encourage girls to become nuns.

Even during his life, miracles began to surround him. At times Gerard Majella was seen rising several feet above the ground during intense prayer. He brought a boy who had fallen from a high cliff back to life. He blessed the small supply of wheat belonging to a poor family, and it lasted until the next harvest.

Once, as he was leaving the home of friends, one of the daughters called after him that he had forgotten his handkerchief. Gerard Majella answered, "Keep it. It will be useful to you some day." A few years later, the girl had married and was in danger of dying in childbirth. She remembered the words of Gerard Majella and called out for the handkerchief. Immediately the danger passed, and she delivered a healthy baby.

Gerard Majella is the patron saint of expectant mothers. In 1941 the League of St. Gerard was founded in Canada to harness the power of prayer to aid mothers in childbirth. Many hospitals throughout the world dedicate their maternity wards to him and give medals and prayer leaflets of St. Gerard to their patients.

*S*aint Isaac Jogues, as you withstood the taunts and torments of unbelievers, help me stand strong when my faith is tested.

Saint Isaac Jogues

Called the "Apostle of the Mohawks," Isaac Jogues was born at Orleans, France, in 1607. His father died soon after Isaac's birth, leaving him to the sole care of his mother. When Isaac was ordained a Jesuit priest, it was to his devout mother that he gave his first priestly blessing and holy communion.

Isaac Jogues went to Canada in 1636 to preach the Gospel to the Indian tribes. He believed that each and every soul is valuable to God. God's grace had blessed his soul, and it was now his duty to bring the souls of others into God's realm. He also was ready to be a martyr for his faith. Not long before, a Jesuit priest named Spinola had been killed in Japan. Isaac Jogues carried a picture of Fr. Spinola with him always.

Jogues and the other French priests made many converts, but some Indians believed the Jesuits were witches who brought famine and sickness. After delivering supplies and medicine to the Huron tribe, Isaac Jogues and several companions were captured by the Mohawk tribe and blamed for a crop failure. They were tortured and put to death in 1646. Isaac Jogues could have escaped, but he chose to face his persecutors and show them that a man of God felt no fear.

"I am a man like yourselves," he told his captors. "I do not fear death or torture. I do not know why you wish to kill me. I come here to confirm the peace and show you the way to heaven."

Isaac Jogues was one of a group of eight missionaries known as the North American Martyrs. Two shrines commemorate their courage. One is at Auriesville, New York; the other is at Midland, Ontario.

*S*aint Paul of the Cross, as you saw in Jesus' suffering the salvation of the human race, help me remember the sacrifice God made for our triumph over evil.

Saint Paul of the Cross *Feast Day: October 20*

*P*aul of the Cross was born in Italy in 1694. Inspired by his mother's teachings, he wanted from an early age to spend his entire life living and preaching the Passion of Christ.

When he was a boy, a heavy bench fell on his foot. Paul ignored the bleeding wound and said it was "a rose sent from God." As a young man, he joined the army to fight the Turks in the hope of dying for his faith. A voice from heaven told him to return home and fight a spiritual war for the souls of humankind.

Paul and his younger brother John founded an order of monks called the Passionists. The Passionists made a special promise to promote the memory of Jesus' passion by preaching and by helping the poor, in whom they see the image of the crucified Christ suffering for humanity's sins. Paul wrote, "The world lives unmindful of the sufferings of Jesus which are the miracle of miracles of the love of God. We must arouse the world from its slumber."

Because of this special devotion to Our Lord, Paul became known as "Paul of the Cross." He traveled for more than forty years, preaching and helping people wherever he went. He was a speaker of such fervency and power that even hardened soldiers and bandits were seen to weep at his words.

Paul of the Cross died at age eighty-one as the Passion was being read to him. Today, there are 2,000 Passionists in 52 nations keeping his dream alive and bearing witness to his credo, "Live in such a way that all may know that you bear outwardly as well as inwardly the image of Christ crucified, the model of all gentleness and mercy."

*S*aint Anthony Claret, you spent your life seeking justice for all God's children. Help me use the Catholic faith to make the world a better place.

Saint Anthony Claret

When Anthony Claret was only five years of age, he was already concerned about his soul being fit for Heaven. The son of a Spanish weaver, Anthony wished to be a priest but obeyed his father instead, who installed him in the family textile business.

But the call of Christ was too great, and Anthony was ordained a priest at age twenty-eight. In 1849 Anthony founded the Congregation of Missionary Sons of the Immaculate Heart of Mary, an order also known as Claretian Missionaries.

Anthony often read *The Lives of the Saints* and was inspired by their example. "I used to feel such a burning within me that I could not sit still," he wrote. "I had to get up and run from one place to another, preaching continually. I thought of the words of St. Augustine, 'Will you not be like these men and women and work as they did at saving souls?'"

He was named Archbishop of Cuba and helped establish hospitals, orphanages, homes for the elderly, trade schools and banks for the poor. Often, he rode on horseback throughout the island to say Mass, and it was said that the rosary was never out of his hands.

One day a madman attacked him with a razor. Anthony's injuries were miraculously healed, and the wound on his arm healed to form an image of Our Lady of Sorrows. The would-be killer was a man whom Anthony had previously helped release from prison. He again interceded for the man and succeeded in having his death sentence reduced to life in prison.

In 1857 Anthony returned to Spain and continued to work on behalf of the poor, even declaring that no one, no matter how poor, was to be turned away from the Catholic hospital in Madrid. Anthony also had the gift of prophecy and performed many miracles before dying in 1870.

*S*aint Jude, you kept the flame of Jesus' Sacred Heart burning bright for all to see. Help me never lose sight of God's goodness and mercy.

Saint Jude

*O*ne of the Twelve Apostles, Jude was a brother of St. James and St. Simon and a cousin of Jesus. At the Last Supper, Jude asked Jesus to show Himself to the whole world after His resurrection, and this has happened many times throughout history.

Jude wrote a short epistle that warned new Christians not to be tempted by false teachings. He wrote, "Now I desire to remind you, though you were once for all fully informed, that He who saved a people out of the land of Egypt, afterward destroyed those who did not believe."

After Jesus ascended into heaven, Jude spread the word of Christ as far as he could travel. He converted many people in Africa, the Middle East and even as far into Asia as the country of Persia, where he and his brother Simon were killed for their faith. At first Jude and Simon were honored by the Persian king, and 60,000 thousand Persians converted to Christianity. But then the people returned to their idols and demanded the brothers be killed.

As they were about to be put to death, Jude and Simon had a vision of Jesus among His angels. Simon said to Jude, "One of the angels has told me, 'I will take you out of the temple and bring the building down upon their heads.'" But Simon told the angel to spare the people in hopes that they would be converted. Even as Jude and Simon were clubbed to death, they blessed God and prayed for their murderers.

Because he often resisted temptation and never wavered on his path to God, Jude is the patron saint of causes that seem hopeless.

*S*aint Martin de Porres, you were given the chance to serve God by helping the sick and poor. Show me ways I can serve God in my daily life.

Saint Martin de Porres

Martin de Porres was born at Lima, Peru, in 1579. His father was a Spanish nobleman, his mother a freed African slave. He grew up very poor and spent much of his youth apprenticed to a barber and surgeon from whom he learned how to care for the sick.

Martin de Porres dreamed of traveling the world and doing great deeds. Instead, he spent his life in his home town of Lima, working in hospitals and serving the poor in a day when medical treatment often was only available to the wealthy.

At age eleven Martin de Porres became a servant in a Dominican abbey. Impressed by his faithful goodness, the abbot gave him the job of alms-seeker. Each day Martin de Porres went out on the streets, begging more than $2,000 each week from the rich to support the poor and sick of Lima.

At fifteen, he became a lay Dominican brother and hoped to become a martyr in a far-off land. Yet, the needs of the people in his home town were very great, and Martin de Porres stayed to help them. He founded an orphanage and helped care for the slaves brought to Peru from Africa. He also started a hospital for cats, dogs and other small animals.

One time Martin de Porres was ordered to set out poison for rats who were troubling the monastery. He obeyed but was very sorry for the rats. He went to the garden and called softly to the rats. They came out of their hiding places, and Martin de Porres scolded them for their bad habits. He said if they would stop bothering the monastery and stayed in the garden, he would feed them every day. From that day forward, there were no rats in the monastery.

Martin de Porres died in Lima in 1639 of fever while serving in his hospital. Canonized in 1962, he was the first American saint of African ancestry. Martin de Porres never traveled the world, but he served God in many ways by serving ordinary people.

*S*aint Charles Borromeo, you spoke the word of God with clarity and truth. Give me the strength to make my voice heard in God's service.

Saint Charles Borromeo

Charles Borromeo was a very moving preacher, even though he had a lifelong speech impediment. When he gave a sermon, those who listened said they did not hear his stutter but instead heard only the pure voice of God.

He was born in 1538 of a wealthy Italian family. Charles Borromeo was a pious youth, and at age twelve entered the Benedictine abbey for his education.

Charles Borromeo was an important figure in the Catholic Reformation. He used his learning and powers of persuasion to defend the Church against heresy. He also worked hard to rid the Catholic Church of the abuses and evils often found among the nobles and clergy of the period. "I admit that we are all weak," he wrote, "but if we want help, the Lord God has given us the means to find it easily. We must meditate before, during and after everything we do. In meditation we find the strength to bring Christ to birth in ourselves and in other men."

As Archbishop of Milan in the 1550s, he started the first children's Sunday school. By the time he died in 1584, there were over 700 schools teaching the principles of the Catholic faith to more than 40,000 students. When a terrible plague broke out in Milan, Charles Borromeo did not leave the stricken city but stayed at the side of the sick. He sold everything in his palace, even his straw mattress, to obtain money for the sick and poor. He built many schools, seminaries and hospitals.

Said Charles Borromeo, "If we wish to make any progress in the service of God, we must begin every day of our life with new eagerness. We must keep ourselves in the presence of God as much as possible and have no other view or end in all our actions but the divine honor."

*M*other Cabrini, you gave comfort and hope to the humblest of God's people. Help me show my care for those who need my aid and solace.

Mother Cabrini Feast Day: November 13

*F*rances Cabrini was born in 1850, one of thirteen children raised on a farm in rural Italy. On the day of her birth a flock of white doves came down from the sky onto her father's land.

As a girl she dreamed of being a missionary to China. She even gave up candies because she would not have them in China. But because she was sickly and was even afflicted with smallpox, no one thought she would ever be strong enough to leave her home village.

Frances Cabrini surprised everyone by becoming a nun and teaching at several Italian orphanages. In 1880, her bishop asked her to found the Missionary Sisters of the Sacred Heart of Jesus. Nine years later, Pope Leo XIII took note of her excellent work and sent her to the United States to help the immigrants who had flocked to America's cities in search of freedom and wealth.

Frances Cabrini and six other Sacred Heart nuns arrived in New York at a time when social aid to the needy was the responsibility of religious and private groups. Within a few years they had founded nearly 70 schools, hospitals, and orphanages in the United States, Europe and South America. Their hard work and Christ-like example encouraged many others to become involved in helping the poor.

Frances Cabrini wrote, "We must pray without tiring, for the salvation of mankind does not depend on material success, nor on sciences that cloud the intellect. Neither does it depend on arms and human industries, but on Jesus alone."

Because she treated thousands of strangers as her own family, Frances Cabrini became known as Mother Cabrini. She died at age sixty-seven, as she was making Christmas presents for one of her orphanages. Mother Cabrini is the first U.S. citizen to be canonized. She is the patron saint of orphans.

*S*aint Gertrude, you loved God with a passion that uplifted the hearts of all who knew you. Inspire me to tell others of Jesus' love for them.

Saint Gertrude

Gertrude was born in 1264 in Saxony and joined the convent when she was very young. She was a good student, but became bored by her studies. One day Jesus appeared to her. He told her that from now on, she need think only of loving Him.

After this, Gertrude studied the Bible with great joy and wrote many beautiful prayers. Her writings were greatly praised in later times by St. Teresa and St. Francis de Sales. Gertrude spent much time praying for sinners and their salvation.

Jesus appeared to St. Gertrude many times. Because of her great love for Him, Jesus gave Gertrude a special vision. He showed her His own Sacred Heart and let her rest her head on His Heart. She wrote, "O Sacred Heart of Jesus, fountain of eternal life, Your Heart is a glowing furnace of Love. You are my refuge and my sanctuary. O my adorable and loving Savior, consume my heart with the burning fire with which Yours is aflamed. Pour down on my soul those graces which flow from Your love. Let my heart be united with Yours. Let my will be conformed to Yours in all things. May Your Will be the rule of all my desires and actions."

On the day she died in 1334, one of the nuns at her side saw Gertrude's soul go straight to the Heart of Jesus, which opened to receive it.

Gertrude is the patron saint of nuns and travelers. Though she died before the European discovery of the New World, she is greatly venerated in North and South America, especially the West Indies and Peru.

*S*aint Rose Philippine Duchesne, fill our hearts with the same pioneering zeal you felt when you took the teachings of Jesus Christ to the other side of the world. Let us also be a source of faith for those we meet throughout our lives.

Saint Rose Philippine Duchesne Feast Day: November 18

Saint Rose Philippine Duchesne was born in 1769 to a wealthy family in Grenoble, France. Even as a child she wanted to preach the Catholic faith in North America, which was then sparsely settled. She began to live like a nun while still in her family home, refusing to wear her beautiful clothing, seeking the most unpleasant of household chores and following a strict routine of daily prayer. At age 19, she joined the Visitation nuns and started a school for poor children.

During the French Revolution many priests and nuns were persecuted. Sister Rose Philippine left the convent and became a teacher. She nursed the sick, found homes for orphans and donated food to the poor. She also helped hide many fugitive priests hiding from the government.

In 1818, as a member of the Sacred Heart nuns, Sister Rose Philippine was sent to North America to do missionary work in the new United States. She built her first mission in St. Charles, Missouri, and established the first free school west of the Mississippi River. Later, she built a convent, an orphanage, a parish school, a school for Indians and a boarding academy.

Sister Rose Philippine cared a great deal about Native Americans and was concerned about the treatment they received from the American government. She spent much time teaching the Indians and trying to get medicine for them. In the Potowatomi language she was known as "Woman-Who-Prays-Always".

One of her favorite prayers was: "O Eternal Father, I come to you through the heart of my Jesus, who is the Way, the Truth, and the Life. Through this divine Heart I adore You for those who do not adore you; I love You for those who do not love you. I gratefully acknowledge You to be my God."

Saint Rose Philippine Duchesne died in 1852 at St. Chartes and was canonized on July 3, 1988 by Pope John Paul II.

*S*aint Cecilia, your prayerful song worked a miracle. Help me use my talents to open people's ears to God's message of love.

Saint Cecilia

*T*he patron saint of music and musicians, Cecilia lived in the second century after Christ. She was the daughter of a wealthy Roman family, who forced her to marry Valerian, a pagan. Dutifully obeying her parents, Cecilia married Valerian but sang a song to God at the wedding, praying her husband might be converted to Christianity.

Cecilia told Valerian that she had an angel by her side, and in order to see it, he must be baptized a Christian. Valerian agreed and converted to Christianity right away. Coming back from his baptism ceremony, he saw his wife in prayer with an angel with flaming wings standing next to her. The angel placed a crown on each of their heads and said Valerian might have a favor from heaven. He asked that his brother, Tiburtius, become a Christian, too. Soon after, Tiburtius was baptized also.

Cecilia, Valerian and Tiburtius gave their family fortune to help the poor of Rome and to aid the families of Christians martyred by the emperor. The two brothers devoted themselves to burying the Christian martyrs killed each day by the pagan Roman authorities.

In the year 177 A.D. Valerian and Tiburtius were themselves arrested and killed for their faith. Soon after, Cecilia was condemned to be suffocated by steam, but she survived and was then beheaded. During her persecution she remained cheerful and managed to convert several of her captors to Christ. Miraculously, when her tomb was opened in 1599, her body was found to be whole.

Much great music has been written celebrating Cecilia, including at least five complete Masses and works by composers such as Friedrich Handel and Henry Purcell. Throughout the world, numerous musical societies performing religious music claim her as their patron and inspiration.

*O*ur Lady of Lavang, you gave your people hope in the face of
unspeakable tragedy. May the faith of the Vietnamese Martyrs inspire
us to stand up for what we believe, even when it is not popular.

Vietnamese Martyred Saints   *Feast Day: November 24*

*E*arly in the 16th century, missionaries from Spain, Portugal, and Holland came to preach the Good News in Vietnam. Because of many complicated social and political reasons, Christianity was rejected and the missionaries and Christians were considered enemies. Over the centuries, the emperors officially issued many edicts to outlaw Catholicism, and imposed punishments including death on the Catholics who would not publicly deny their faith.

The suffering of the Vietnamese Catholics reached its zenith during 1885 to 1886. In only a few months, nearly 60,000 Catholics were executed. This number nearly equaled the total of the two previous centuries.

During the periods of persecution, a total of 53 royal edicts forbidding Christianity were published. Each time an edict was enacted, the storm of persecution renewed itself: churches, convents, seminaries, parochial schools, religious papers, and other possessions of the Catholics were burnt or torn down. Many Catholics were imprisoned, tortured, or killed, while others took refuge in thick forests or remote islands. Many horrible forms of torture were invented to execute Catholics. About 130,000 Vietnamese Catholics were killed during this period. Of this number, 117 were canonized by Pope John Paul II on June 19, 1988. These suffering Martyrs came from all walks of life: 8 Bishops, 50 Priests (37 Vietnamese and 13 Missionaries), 16 Evangelists, 1 Seminarian, 42 Lay Persons (41 men and 1 woman). In 1798, the Blessed Virgin Mary appeared at Lavang to encourage and strengthen her children in their suffering and misery.

The 117 Martyred Saints, as well as the nearly 130,000 Catholics who suffered death, are heroic witnesses of faith, and loyal disciples of Christ. The headquarters of the Vietnamese religious order CMC and the Vietnamese Martyrs Center is located in Carthage, Missouri.

*S*aint Catherine Labouré, you showed us the love Mary has for her children. Help me know the Blessed Virgin's power to bring blessings into my life.

Saint Catherine Labouré *Feast Day: November 28*

*C*atherine Labouré was the ninth of eleven children and grew up on a farm in France in the early 1800s. When she was nine years old, her mother died. From that time on, Catherine sought solace in her heavenly mother, the Blessed Virgin. She prayed that someday she would see Mary.

One day she visited a hospital run by the Sisters of Charity. Catherine received a vision of Saint Vincent de Paul, who told her that God wanted her to work with the sick. Believing this was indeed the will of God, Catherine joined the Sisters of Charity.

In 1830 Catherine was kneeling in the convent chapel when she saw the Blessed Virgin Mary appear in all her glory. Mary pointed to the altar and told Catherine this was the source of all consolation for humankind.

A few months later, the Blessed Virgin again appeared and told Catherine to have a special medal made that would spread devotion to the Mother of God. The medal was to have the image of Our Lady, and the words, "O Mary, conceived without sin, pray for us who have recourse to thee" on one side. The other side was to bear an image of the hearts of Jesus and Mary. The Blessed Virgin told Catherine that wearers of the medal would receive great graces.

Catherine told only her confessor, a priest who consulted the Archbishop of Paris. The Archbishop gave permission to create the medal in 1832. The first medals were made and were very popular. Many miracles of grace, health, peace and prosperity occurred to those who wore it. Before long people were calling it the "Miraculous Medal."

Catherine spent the rest of her life caring for the elderly in her town and working to let the world know how to summon the power of Mary's aid.

*S*aint Andrew, you were among the first to see the wonder of Christ hidden among earthly things. Help me find the true purpose of my life in God's work.

Saint Andrew
Feast Day: November 30

*T*he patron saint of Russia and Scotland and of fishermen, Andrew was the first disciple of Jesus. Like his brother, Simon Peter, Andrew was a fisherman in Galilee, working hard every day to earn a living from the sea. One day Andrew saw Jesus pass by and began walking behind Him, knowing in his heart that this was no ordinary man but the long-awaited Messiah.

Andrew told his brother he should also follow Jesus, but Simon Peter warned they must not give up their work. Jesus turned and said to them, "Follow Me and I will make you fishers of men." Both brothers decided to dedicate their lives to spreading the word of God. They followed Jesus from that day forward.

One day, in the hills above the Sea of Tiberias, a huge crowd of 5,000 people came to see Jesus and the Apostles. Jesus asked Philip how they would be able to feed so many people. Andrew stepped forward and said, "There is a a boy here who has five barley loaves and two fish. But what are they among so many?" Jesus multiplied this meager offering and fed the crowd. With this miracle he proved that belief in the power of God can overcome any earthly condition.

Following the Resurrection, Andrew helped establish the new Christian faith in Israel. He then traveled for many years preaching in Scythia and Greece until he was crucified in Achaia during the reign of the Emperor Nero. Today, the Society of St. Andrew is a ministry that fights hunger in America by saving fresh produce that would otherwise go to waste and giving it to the needy.

*S*aint Francis Xavier, you boldly took the words of Jesus to the farthest reaches of the earth. Show me how to live those words in my daily life.

Saint Francis Xavier

*T*rained as a philosopher, Francis Xavier of Spain was one of the greatest missionaries ever known. In ten years of preaching in India, Japan and the East Indies during the 1540s, he baptized more than 40,000 souls. He sought out the poor and forgotten, bringing them the hopeful message of Jesus Christ.

He wrote to St. Ignatius Loyola, "Many, many people hereabouts are not becoming Christians for one reason only — there is nobody to make them Christians. I have not stopped since the day I arrived. I conscientiously made the rounds of the villages. I bathed in the sacred waters all the children who had not yet been baptized. This means that I have purified a very large number of children so young that, as the saying goes, they could not tell their right hand from their left. The older children would not let me say my Office or eat or sleep until I taught them one prayer or another. Then I began to understand: 'The kingdom of heaven belongs to such as these.'"

Francis was not afraid to talk about God's commandments to even the most powerful of men. He criticized the King of Portugal about the slave trade. Said Francis to the King, "You have no right to spread the Catholic faith while you take away all the country's riches. It upsets me to know that at the hour of your death, you may be ordered out of paradise."

Francis had the gift of tongues, and there are many stories of his healing miracles and ability to calm storms and raise the dead. In Japan, he filled the Sea of Cangoxima with fish after it had been barren of marine life for years.

Francis Xavier died in China of malaria in 1552. He is the patron saint of missionaries and navigators.

*S*aint Barbara, even the most severe isolation could not keep you from reaching out to God. Help me to always see God wherever I am.

Saint Barbara
Feast Day: December 4

Barbara lived in the third century and was raised by pagan parents near Nicomedia in Asia Minor. She was very beautiful, and her father, Dioscorus, kept her locked in a luxurious tower. He wanted to make sure she would marry only a man he thought best for her.

Yet, Dioscorus allowed her to be taught by poets and philosophers, and it was from these teachers that Barbara learned about Jesus Christ and the new Christian religion. Two Christian friends, Origen and Valentinian, helped her secretly convert.

Despite the cruel treatment she suffered from her misguided parents, Barbara's new-found faith made her happy. She even re-designed a building her father was building for her to reflect her new religion. Instead of the two windows her father had ordered, Barbara had three windows put in the building, as a symbol of the Holy Trinity.

When she came of age to marry, her father urged her to find a suitor. Barbara wanted to remain of service to her parents and did not want to marry. She also had been baptized as a Christian and wanted to dedicate her life to Christ. When she told this to her father, he denounced her to the civil tribunal that persecuted Christians. Barbara was horribly tortured and finally beheaded along with another Christian girl named Juliana.

God quickly punished her persecutors. As her soul was being borne by angels to heaven, a flash of lightning struck Dioscorus and killed him instantly. At the grave where Barbara and Juliana were buried, miracles began to occur that healed the sick. Today, Barbara is a patron saint of protection against fire and lightning and sudden death.

*S*aint Nicholas, you spent your life doing good works for God's poor. Help me be generous to the needy of my world, especially those lacking in faith and hope.

Saint Nicholas *Feast Day: December 6*

*N*icholas was born of a wealthy family in Asia Minor around 280 A.D. When his parents died, Nicholas used his inheritance to help the poor. He became the bishop of Myra and made sure the Church shared its riches with the needy. Many stories of his generosity have come to us through the centuries.

Once, he learned that a family was so poor, the father planned to sell his daughters into slavery. During the next three nights, Nicholas secretly threw bags of gold into the house — one for each daughter — to pay the debt and save the daughters.

Another time Nicholas brought back to life three young boys who had been murdered and hidden in a barrel of brine to hide the terrible crime. While on a sea voyage to the Holy Land, a fierce storm threatened to sink the ship on which Nicholas was sailing. Nicholas prayed, and the storm calmed immediately.

Nicholas also saved three innocent men from an unjust execution by the Emperor Constantine, who heard Nicholas' prayers in a dream and knew God had spoken through the holy bishop. Nicholas was said to have frequently persuaded thieves to return what they stole. For this reason he is a patron saint of thieves who repent and want to become just.

After Nicholas died in 342, many other stories arose of his generosity, especially to children. These stories form the modern legend of Santa Claus, another kindly gift-giver who reveals the limitless bounty in store for every Child of God.

More than twelve hundred churches around the world have been dedicated in Nicholas' honor. By the Middle Ages, his feast day of December 6 had become a special day for people to show generosity to friends and family. It is still celebrated in many European countries such as Holland, Germany and Switzerland as a means of preparing for the Christmas season and the coming of Jesus Christ, who gave humankind the gift of Eternal Life.

$\mathcal{S}$aint Juan Diego, you greeted Blessed Mother Mary upon her arrival in the New World. Intercede with her so that we can know her motherly kindness and compassion.

Saint Juan Diego

Saint Juan Diego was born in 1474 in the province of Cuauhtitlan, about 15 miles north of modern Mexico City. He was of native Chichimeca ancestry, and his name in the Náhuatl language means "eagle that talks".

After the Spanish conquered Mexico in 1521, Juan Diego converted to Catholicism. He was a simple man who worked as a mat maker and farm laborer. On the morning of December 9, 1531 he was on his way to Mass when the Blessed Virgin Mary appeared and announced herself to him at a place called Tepeyac. She asked Juan Diego to tell the Bishop that a shrine be built at that spot.

Juan Diego was astonished by what he had seen and heard. He went to Bishop and relayed the Blessed Mother's request. The Bishop did not believe Juan Diego and asked for proof that what he said had happened was true. Three days later, Juan Diego returned to Tepeyac. The Blessed Mother told him to climb a hill and pick the flowers that were in bloom.

Even though it was winter time, Juan Diego found roses blooming. Our Lady told him to take them to the Bishop as proof. When Juan Diego opened his cloak to show the roses to the Bishop, the flowers fell on the ground and an image of the Blessed Mother appeared on the cloak, exactly as Juan Diego had described her.

The Bishop built a church where the Blessed Virgin had directed, and this church is known today as the Basilica of Guadalupe in honor of the name given to Mary as she appeared in the Americas —the Virgin of Guadalupe. Juan Diego's cloak is in the church, and the image of Mary has not faded over the centuries.

Juan Diego lived the rest of his life as a hermit in a small hut near the basilica. Here he cared for the church and the first pilgrims who came to pray to the Mother of Jesus. Juan Diego died in 1548 and was canonized on July 31, 2002 by Pope John Paul II.

$\mathcal{S}$aint Lucy, you never lost your faith in the power of God's mercy. Help me use my vision to see the works of Jesus in my daily life.

Saint Lucy

*L*ucy lived in the fourth century in Sicily. Her name means "light" in Latin and is related to the word "lucid," which means "radiant, clear and understandable."

When her mother became very ill, Lucy helped her make a pilgrimage to the shrine of St. Agatha. Lucy and her mother prayed by the shrine for many hours before falling asleep. Suddenly, St. Agatha appeared to Lucy. She told Lucy her mother would be cured and that Lucy would someday be a martyr for her faith. The next morning, Lucy's mother awoke completely cured.

A few years later, a pagan man wanted to marry Lucy. She wanted to remain a virgin and serve only God. The man was furious at her refusal and brought soldiers to kill her. When the soldiers tried to move her, they could not do so. They harnessed Lucy to bulls, but she could still not be moved. The soldiers covered her in oil and started a fire, but it did not burn her. Her eyes were torn out, but she still refused to abandon her faith. Finally, she was stabbed with a sword and died, as the vision of St. Agatha had predicted.

Before Lucy died, her sight was miraculously restored. For this reason, she is the patron of the blind and those suffering from eye diseases.

Lucy is a favorite saint of many around the world. In Sweden her feast day of December 13 is one of the shortest days of the year in the middle of winter. The Swedes celebrate this change of season with a Festival of Light. On this day the youngest daughter dresses in white and wears a crown of lit candles. She wakes the rest of the family with coffee, rolls and a special song. In other European countries young girls walk through their neighborhood holding candles and singing carols.

$\mathcal{S}$aint Stephen, as you courageously spread the Savior's message, help me speak God's truth when I am called upon.

Saint Stephen

Feast Day: December 26

Stephen was the first Christian martyr. He was killed simply for speaking the new truth of Jesus.

Stephen was one of the seven deacons the Apostles named to carry out works of charity. Stephen was brought before the tribunal of chief priests in Jerusalem and accused of blasphemy. Stephen told them Jesus was the Messiah that Israel had long awaited and that they should follow His path.

The tribunal was enraged and ordered Stephen to be killed. He was taken outside and stoned to death. As he died, he called out, "Lord Jesus, receive my spirit!" With his last breath of life and in imitation of Jesus' last words on the cross, Stephen asked God to forgive his killers, saying, "Lord, do not lay this sin against them!"

Stephen's cousin, Saul, was in the crowd watching. Stephen prayed for Saul to see the error of his ways, and shortly after Saul — now known as Paul — received his conversion on the road to Damascus.

Stephen is the patron saint of horses, and there are many customs related to Stephen's feast day of December 26. For centuries, people in Europe have decorated their horses on this day and brought them to church to be blessed by the priest. In Sweden, stable boys are blessed in a special ceremony. In Poland, the horses' food is blessed and special horseshoe-shaped bread is baked and eaten. In the British Isles, Stephen's feast is called Wren Day and plays celebrating the triumph of Christianity over pagan gods are performed. And in the popular Christmas song, Good King Wenceslas, the King carries on the tradition of Stephen's good works by taking food to the poor on Stephen's feast day.

*S*aint John, you stood by Jesus whenever He needed you. Guide Jesus to me when I need Him at my side.

Saint John

Feast Day: December 27

John was one of the original disciples. He experienced the wonder of living each day with Jesus. He traveled everywhere with Jesus and saw Jesus perform many miracles. John was present at the Last Supper and was the only disciple who did not leave Jesus during His death on the cross.

John had a very good memory of all these events, and his Gospel offers a vivid account of Jesus' life. He also wrote three Epistles and the Book of the Apocalypse.

In the Gospel of John, the divine part of Jesus' nature is highlighted. Jesus tells the disciples, "Before Abraham was, I am." And He declares, "I am the way, and the truth, and the life."

The Jewish religion as seen in the Old Testament was a religion of hope: when God the Father revealed Himself through His Messiah, the world would be one step closer toward Paradise. Many of the early Christians had been Jews and held this unique belief in future salvation. The Gospel of John shows that Jesus is not only the Jewish Messiah, but the Son of God and Messiah for all humankind.

Many miracles surround John. Tradition says he was once thrown into a cauldron of boiling oil but stepped out unharmed. Another time, unbelievers tried to stone him, but the rocks turned and hit the throwers. He cast out a demon from a pagan temple and fire from heaven struck down two hundred idol worshippers. John raised the dead worshippers, and they were baptized immediately.

For his faithfulness to Jesus, John is known as "the beloved disciple." He died in the second century at age ninety-four and is the patron saint of writers.

Prayer to My Patron Saint

You lived a blessed life devoted to making the world a more divine place. Help me see the truth of God's teachings with every breath I take. Share with me your wisdom, compassion, and love of all things good. Give me courage to follow the way of Christ and never lose my belief in the power of His miracles. Guide my steps so they lead directly to God, and use your heavenly influence to keep me in God's goodness and mercy until the day we meet in Paradise. I give myself into your care. Amen.